£3·00
£2·00

EVERYDAY LIFE

IN

ANGLO-SAXON
VIKING

AND

NORMAN TIMES

Fig. 1.   The Anglo-Saxon Hall (*imaginary reconstruction*)

EVERYDAY LIFE IN ANGLO-SAXON, VIKING, AND NORMAN TIMES

WRITTEN AND ILLUSTRATED BY
MARJORIE & C.H.B.QUENNELL, AUTHORS
OF "EVERYDAY THINGS IN ENGLAND"
LONDON
B.T.BATSFORD LTD., 94 HIGH HOLBORN

" He was affable and pleasant to all,
and curiously eager to investigate things unknown."

From *Life of King Alfred*, by Asser.

First Edition, MCMXXVI.
Made and printed in Great Britain by
Fleetway Press, Ltd., London.

CONTENTS

PAGE

FOREWORD – – – – – – – vi

SHORT LIST OF AUTHORITIES – – – vii

CHART – – – – – – – – viii

CHAPTER

I. THE COMING OF THE ENGLISH – – 1

Roman Britain—Saxon Raids—The Saxons—The
Conquest of the Britons—Anglo-Saxon Character-
istics — Clothes — Brooches—Weaving—Ecclesiasti-
cal Dress—Saxon England—Saxon Houses—Beo-
wulf—Halls—Timber Framing—German Houses—
Mensuration—Household Gear—Burial—Medicine—
Education — Literature — Giants — Manuscripts —
Writing — Christianity — S. Patrick — Augustine —
Paulinus — Temples — Aidan — Wilfrid — British
Christians.

II. THE COMING OF THE VIKINGS – – 56

The Viking Ship—Vikings on Land—Viking Gods—
Alfred—Travels—Alfred's Ships—Building—Saxon
Decline—Church Building—Bells—Christian Sym-
bols — Monasticism — Church Dues — Eorles and
Ceorles.

III. THE COMING OF THE NORMANS – – 90

Master Wace—Harold's Oath—Norman Landing—
Castles—Shell Keep—Norman House—Chessmen—
Norman Church—Vaulting.

INDEX TO TEXT AND ILLUSTRATIONS – 113

FOREWORD

THIS book completes a cycle which started with the Norman Conquest in Part I of a *History of Everyday Things in England*, and, swinging round by way of the Old Stone Age, in Part I of the " Everyday Life " Series has, with this Part IV, reached the starting point again. The theme of the six books has been the interest of creative work We have endeavoured to show man at work, feeding, clothing, and housing himself.   We have tried to indicate the difficulties he has had to overcome, and how he has harnessed the powers of Nature to assist him. It has not been possible to do more than present an outline plan, something which might suggest to the boys and girls for whom we write that here there were paths worth exploring by themselves, or occupations in which they could find pleasure.   Beyond this there is little to say.

Our publisher, Mr. Harry Batsford, has helped us throughout by his interest, and Mr. Reginald Smith, F.S.A., Deputy-Keeper of the Department of British and Mediaeval Antiquities at the British Museum, has very kindly read through our MS., and given us a feeling of security in the presentation of our facts.

MARJORIE AND C. H. B. QUENNELL.

BERKHAMSTED, HERTS.
September, 1926.

TITLE OF BOOK.	AUTHOR.	PUBLISHER.
The Arts in Early England . . .	G. Baldwin Brown, Vol. 1	Murray, 1903.
	G. Baldwin Brown, Vol. 2	Murray, 1925.
	G. Baldwin Brown, Vols. 3 & 4	Murray, 1915.
	G. Baldwin Brown, Vol. 5	Murray, 1921.
Guide to Anglo-Saxon Antiquities .		British Museum, 1923.
A Guide to Early Christian and Byzantine Antiquities		British Museum, 1921.
Origin of Christian Church Art .	Josef Strzygowski	Clarendon Press, 1923.
The Venerable Bede's Ecclesiastical History of England	Ed. by J. A. Giles	George Bell & Sons, 1878.
The Anglo-Saxon Chronicle . .	Ed. by J. A. Giles	George Bell & Sons, 1914.
William of Malmesbury's Chronicle of the Kings of England	Ed. by J. A. Giles	George Bell & Sons, 1911.
The Story of Burnt Njal . .	G. W. Dasent	J. M. Dent & Sons, Ltd., 1911.
Six Old English Chronicles . .	J. A. Giles	Henry G. Bohn, 1848.
Master Wace—His Chronicle of the Norman Conquest	Edgar Taylor	Pickering, 1837.
The Bayeux Tapestry . . .	F. R. Fowke	George Bell & Sons, 1898.
Beowulf	J. R. Clark Hall	Swan, Sonnenschein & Co., 1911.
King Alfred's A.S. Version of the Compendious History of the World	By Orosius (Bosworth)	Simpson, Brown, Green & Simpson, 1859
The Evolution of the English House .	S. O. Addy	Grant Allen & Co., 1910.
The Development of English Building Construction	C. F. Innocent	Cambridge University Press, 1916.
Medieval or "Tithe" Barns. .	Francis B. Andrews	Privately printed.
Scandinavian Britain . . .	W. G. Collingwood	S.P.C.K., 1908.
History of the Norwegian People .	Gjerset	The Macmillan Co., New York, 1915.
The Viking Age	Paul B Du Chaillu	John Murray, 1880.
The Viking Ship	N. Nicolaysen	Alb. Cammermeyer (Christiania), 1882.
Denkmale einer ausgebildeten Holzbaukunst in Norwegens		J. C. C. Dahl, 1837.
The Miniatures and Ornaments of A.S. and Irish Manuscripts . .	Westwood	Quaritch, 1868.
The Book of Kells . . .	Edward Sullivan	*The Studio*, 1920.
Illuminated Manuscripts . .	J. A. Herbert	Methuen & Co., 1911.
Fonts and Font Covers . . .	Francis Bond	Oxford University Press, 1908.
Readings in Social History . .	R. B. Morgan	Cambridge University Press, 1921.

802	Egberht, King of Wessex. d. 837.		... Final conquest of British.	Style ... ment intro ... Irela ... In	Historia Brittonum (Nennius), abt. 800.
828		Arabs begin conquest of Sicily.	Supremacy of Ecgberht.		
837			Defeat of Danes by Ecgberht		
839	Æthelwulf, King of Wessex. d. 858				
849			Birth of Ælfred.	Baldwin Brown B period.	
851			Defeat of Danes at Aclea.		
857	Æthelbald, Kingof Wessex. d. 860.				
860	Æthelberht, King of Wessex. d. 866.				
866	Æthelred, King of Wessex. d. 871		866 Danes land in East Anglia.	Art becomes Scandinavian in the N.	Abt. 868 Martyrdom of Eadmund.
867			Danes conquer Northumbria and capture York.		S. Michael's Church, S. Albans.
870			Danes invade East Anglia and Wessex, 871.		
871	Ælfred, King of Wessex. d. 901.				
878			Ælfred wins battle at Edington—Peace of Wedmore — the Danelaw = Northumbria—half Mercia and E. Anglia.		
897			Alfred builds a Fleet.		Anglo-Saxon Chronicle compiled 891-2.
901	Eadward the Elder.				
912			Northmen attack Normandy.		Deerhurst Church, Glos.
925	Æthelstan. d. 940.				
940	Eadmund. d. 946.				
943			Dunstan, Abbot of Glastonbury.	Baldwin Brown C period.	
946	Eadred. d. 955.				S. Albans, abt. 950.
955	Eadwig. d. 959.		954 Submission of Danelaw —England becomes one kingdom.		
958	Eadgar. d. 975.				Beowulf, about 1000.
975	Eadward the Martyr. d. 978.		959 Dunstan Archbishop of Canterbury.		
978	Æthelred the Unready. d. 1016.	987-1040 Fulk the Black, Count of Anjou.	Benedictine rule introduced. 991 Vikings defeat East Anglians at Maldon.		Worth Church, Sussex. Barnack Church, Northants.
1016	Eadmund Ironside. d. 1016.		1013 England submits to Swein.		Bradford-on-Avon Church, Wilts.
1016	Cnut. d. 1035.		1027 Birth of William of Normandy.		Breamore Church, Hants.
1037	Harald. d. 1040.	1040-60 Geoffry Martel, Count of Anjou.			Earls Barton Church, Northants. S. Benet Church, Cambridge.
1042	Eadward the Confessor. d. 1066.		1054-6 Normans conquer S. Italy and invade Sicily, 1060.		Sompting Church, Sussex.
1051		William of Normandy visits England.			Bosham Church, Sussex.
		1060-90 Normans conquer Sicily.	1060-1080 Close of paganism in Scandinavia.		1054 The Greek Church secedes from Roman Church.
1066	Harold. William the Conqueror.		Harold defeats Hardrada at Stamford Bridge and is defeated himself at Senlac.		1070 Lanfranc, Archbishop of Canterbury, reorganizes Church. 1086 Domesday Book completed.

Table: Chronological synopsis (A.D. 603–796)

Year	English Kings	European / Frankish Events	English Political Events	Church, Art & Culture
603			Battle of Daegsastan.	Paulinus converts Northumbria.
613	Eadwine, King of Northumbria. d. 633.	614 Persians take Jerusalem.	Battle of Chester. Conversion of Eadwine.	
617	Penda, King of Mercians. d. 655.		Supremacy of Eadwine.	
626				
627	Oswald, King of Bernicia. d. 642.		633 Eadwine killed at Hatfield by Mercians. Defeat of Welsh by Oswald.	
635		634-40 Mohammedans conquer Egypt and Syria.	Conversion of Wessex.	635 Aidan goes to Holy Island.
651	Oswiu, King of Northumbria. d. 670.	651 Mohammedans conquer Persia		
655			Battle at Winwaed. W. Saxons invade to the Parret	
658				
659	Wulfhere, King of Mercia.		W. Saxons retreat across Thames.	Caedmon at Whitby.
661				673 Birth of Bede.
664			Council of Whitby.	
668	Ecgfrith, King of Northumbria. d. 685.		Theodore of Tarsus Arch. of Canterbury.	Brixworth Ch., Northants. Wing Church, Bucks. S. Pancras Ch., Canterbury. Bewcastle and Ruthwell Crosses 670-80. Crypt at Hexham.
670	Æthelred, King of Mercia. d. 704.		Completion of English conversion. Now S. Saxons embrace Christianity under Wilfrid, heathen burials cease.	
675				
681				
682	Ine, King of W. Saxons. d. 726.		Death of S. Cuthbert. 687.	Escomb Church, Durham. Franks Casket abt. 700 (Northumbria).
688			Conquest of Mid-Somerset by Wessex.	
715	Æthelbald, King of Mercia. d. 757.	709 Mohammedans conquer N. Africa. 711 Overthrow of Visigoths in Spain by Mohammedans.	Defeat of Mercia by W. Saxons.	Bede, the first English historian, revives classical learning and writes his Ecclesiastical History abt. 730.
716			Mercia conquers Wessex.	Death of Bede.
733		732 Mohammedans defeated at Poitiers by Charles Martel.		Death of Boniface.
735	Offa, King of Mercia. d. 796.	751 The Austrasian Pepin founds Carolingian dynasty.		
753				
754		Emperor Charlemagne (771-814) governs all W. Europe except Spain. Tours on the Loire and Aachen on the Rhine the centres. Beginning of the Holy Roman Empire, 781.	Wessex wins Battle of Burford.	
758				
775		Alcuin of York at the court of Charlemagne.	Mercia subdues Kent.	779 Offa's Dyke. First arrival of Danes.
787				
796	Cenwulf, King of Mercia. d. 821.			793 Foundation of S. Alban's Monastery.

The Franks from Germany conquered Gaul: reached the Somme about ... Gallo-Roman kingdom, under Syagrius, 486. They conquered the Visi... of Italy, and forced them into Spain in 507. Clovis, their leader, was b... kingdom, stretching from Saxony and Bavaria down to Spain. This was div... and Germany.

Prof. Baldwin Brown A period.

Style II. The animal motive develops into elaborate interlacing in decoration. Scandinavian in origin.

III was a Scandinavian development— Vine scroll and figure sculpture used probably by Theodore. In ...d the books of Darrow and Kells. The Lindisfarne orthumbria Gospels (698-721).

CHART

ENGLISH KINGS.	FOREIGN KINGS AND HISTORY	EVENTS	THE CHURCH, ARCHITECTURE AND LITERATURE.
410 Roman protection withdrawn.	429 Vandals invade Africa.	Coming of Hengest, 449.	Roman toleration of Christianity 313.
who had marched into Gaul after their invasion ptized in 496. The Franks founded the Merovingian ded into Neustria and Austrasia, to become later France 430, the Seine 480, and the Loire by 489. Overthrew	451 Defeat of Attila at Châlons.	English conquer Kent, 457.	S. Patrick goes to Ireland about 437.
	Death of Childeric (father of Clovis) 481. Ostrogoths invade Italy 493-553.	Arrival of S. Saxons. Fall of Anderida (Pevensey), 491. Arrival of S. Saxons, 495.	The legend of Arthur may rest on a British king who resisted the Saxon invaders bet. 467-93.
519 Cerdic and Cynric (kings of W. Saxons).	Slavs from N.E., of Carpathians moved W. to Mark of Brandenburg 512.		ment. of applied orna- carving " style 500-550 " Chip-
520 Ida, King of Bernicia. 547 552	546 Rome taken by Goths. Justinian Emperor in the E. 527-565.	Britons win battle at Mount Badon. W. Saxons take Old Sarum (near Salisbury).	De Excidio—Gildas 545-6.
560 Æthelberht, King of Kent, d. 616.	Lombards from Baltic invade Italy.	Æthelbert defeated by W. Saxons.	553 The Silkworm introduced from the East. S. Columba goes to Iona abt. 563.
568		W. Saxons invade Mid-Britain.	
571		" win battle at Deorham.	Abt. 570 Birth of Mahomet at Mecca.
577		" defeated at Faddiley.	
584 Æthelric, King of Northumbria. 588			motive in decoration. -600 Style I of animal
593 Æthelfrith, King of Northumbria, d. 617. 597 Rædwald King of E.		Landing of Augustine	Augustine restores S. Mar-

EVERYDAY LIFE IN ANGLO-SAXON, VIKING & NORMAN TIMES

CHAPTER I

THE COMING OF THE ENGLISH

PART IV of the Series deals with a very interesting period of our history. We begin with the arrival of the men who gave us the right to call ourselves English, and then we show how they were harried by the Vikings, and finally conquered by the Norsemen, Northmen, or Normans. We have grouped the English, Viking, and Norman together, because all were members of the great Nordic race of which we wrote in Part II, on page 9. They were tall and strong, with fair hair, blue eyes, and long heads, and they were all first-rate fighting men. When an Englishman to-day is moved to sing in his bath that Britons never will be slaves, or talks of the British Commonwealth of Nations, he must puzzle the shades of the first Englishmen. When Bede, the historian of the Anglo-Saxons, wrote of the Britons, he meant the people in England before the Saxon Occupation, and they were not all of one race. Asser, writing in the time of Alfred, of Offa's Dyke, describes it as " a great rampart made from sea to sea between Britain (meaning Wales) and Mercia." In Parts I, II and III we have written of the Cro-magnon men, almost as modern in type as ourselves, appearing in Europe in the Old Stone Age ; and in the New Stone, Bronze, and Early Iron Ages, before the Roman Occupation, we have Mediterranean man, followed by the Celtic Gael and Brython (from whom we get the name of Briton), followed by the Belgae. The English did not kill all the Britons ; many

1   B

moved into the West, and others were enslaved and perhaps gained their freedom at a later date, when their children, and their children's children, came to call themselves English.

Roman Britain

An Englishman may conceivably be a descendant of any of the races we have been writing about. A family may come to an end, but it would take a very wise man to say when his own began. This is just as it should be, and it will make our history more intimate ; the people we read about are not pale ghosts, but our ancestors.

Before we tell of the doings of the English, it may be well to hark back a little to Roman Britain. In our last book we tried to give our readers some idea of the great advances which were made then. We saw how the inhabitants of Silchester had town-planned their city ; how the roads which crossed it led to the civic centre, where the Basilica and Forum were ; that it was provided with an inn, public baths, temples, and in the end a Christian Church. We noted that its houses were conveniently planned and scientifically heated.

The word civilization comes from *civis*, a citizen, and a civilized man, in the Roman way of thinking, was a good citizen, in distinction to the *paganus*, or peasant, who was a rougher and more pagan type. If by a wave of some magic wand Silchester, or *Calleva Atrebatum*, the Town in the Wood of the Atrebates, could be rebuilt on its old foundations, and we could walk along its streets, we should have to admit that it was a very civilized place. If we made friends with any of its inhabitants, and asked them to come to see our own town, and if our town dated from the Industrial Revolution, we should have to think of desperate excuses to explain away the slums and squalor, dirt and ugliness, and lack of all plan ; but Silchester lies buried in the pleasant country between Reading and Basingstoke, and its inhabitants sleep without their city walls. Our task is concerned with the everyday life of their immediate successors ; but unless we bear in our mind this picture of Roman Britain, we shall hardly appreciate the terrible desolation which the English wrought here in England.

Saxon Raids

Let us imagine a band of Saxons raiding up the Thames until they came to Reading, and then striking down to the south to Silchester. The inhabitants of the city, warned by fugitives, fled to the west, taking with them their lighter

2

Fig. 2.—Symbol of S. Mark. (Gospels of S. Chad.)

valuables, but burying in wells, as we saw in Part III, page 56, their tools for use when they returned. The Saxons came up to a deserted town, and entering by one of the gates, wandered up and down the paved streets, and in and out of the houses. Joyful shouts went up, that what they had heard was true ; here was a fat land, and loot undreamed of. Warriors staggered out of the shops, their arms full of fine cloths or household gear, and the houses were searched for food and drink. Here the Saxon would have been disappointed, because the Romano-Briton supped in his Triclinium off poultry and vegetable dishes, and liked his food to be set on the table in good red Samian ware, and the raised hearths of their kitchens were not adapted for roasting large joints. The Saxon was a great meat eater. When the Society of Antiquaries were excavating at Silchester, they found a beautiful mosaic floor which was disfigured by a large patch where a fire had been made ; perhaps this was where the Saxons roasted the beast they could not cook in any other way.

Their hunger appeased, they wandered over the city, and coming to the Christian church wondered, as pagans, what were its uses ; perhaps they kicked over the altar to see if there was any treasure under it. Others went to the baths, which, as we saw in Part III, page 25, were large and well planned, and here they splashed about in the cold pool of the Frigidarium, and then, going outside, discovered the elaborate system of heating by fires under the hollow floors.

3

FIG. 3.—Symbol of S. Matthew.
(Gospels of S. Chad.)

Peering under they may have discovered some unfortunate not well enough to escape, and dragged him out to be made sport with, and then killed. Skeletons have been discovered, in hypocausts, of people who hid in this way.

The elaborate organization of a city ; the details of its water supply, and sanitation, and its maintenance, were entirely beyond the comprehension of the Saxons ; it was then, just as if to-day, a stranded aeroplane were found by a party of Australian black men ; they would play with it, and steal the gadgets, and then tire of it and go away. This is what the Saxons did at Silchester ; the town does not appear to have been destroyed by fire, but left to moulder into ruin after the raiders moved on to find fresh fields to conquer.

The Saxons We will now find out something about these Angles, Saxons, and Jutes who worked such changes in our country, and we cannot do better than refer to the writings of the Venerable Bede. Bede was born in 673, and was placed, at the age of 7, with Abbot Biscop in the Abbey of Wearmouth.

He was a student all his days, and helped to revive classical learning, and by writing his Ecclesiastical History, about 730, became the first English historian. Bede, writing of the invaders, said : "Those who came over were of the three most powerful nations of Germany — Saxons, Angles, and Jutes," they called themselves *Angelcyn*, the

FIG. 4.—Symbol of S. Mark.
(Gospels of S. Chad.)

4

English nation. It must be remembered that the invasion of our country was only a minor detail in a much larger movement of men.

We saw in Part II, page 75, and Fig. 64, how the dust blown by great blizzards from the moraines of glaciers in the Ice Ages, was deposited as Loess, and formed the grasslands which spread in a broad zone across Europe from the Ural Mountains to the

Fig. 5.—Symbol of S. Luke. (Gospels of S. Chad.)

North of France. The central Asian Plains always have been the breeding places of masses of men, who at times, moved perhaps by drought, break their bounds and surge outwards, and the grasslands have afforded them a path. It should be remembered that the Beaker men arrived here in England from South Russia on this same path, Part II, page 11. The Anglo-Saxons came to England as a result of disturbance in Central Asia. The Huns came from there, and attacked their neighbours, the Goths, who moved across the Danube, and the Rhine, into the Roman Empire. The Goths captured Rome, and sacked it in 410, and the movement was not stopped until Attila, the King of the Huns, was defeated at Châlons in 451. Another Teutonic people, the Franks, moved into France for the same reason and reached the Loire by 489.

"Westward Ho" is a very old cry, but in the days of which we are writing it was one fraught with awful peril for civilization. The Roman Empire spelled civilization, and

Fig. 6.—Symbol of S. John. (Gospels of S. Chad.)

5

FIG. 7.—Figure from Book of Kells.

it was a wonderful fabric The Empire was bounded by the Danube, and the Rhine, and across these rivers surged hordes of pagan barbarians, as in older days still the Achaeans had borne down on the Mycenaeans in Greece.

Very truly the historians talk of the Dark Ages; yet through the Darkness come flashes. If we know little of the period, yet what is known is always coloured by life and movement. On one page we shall have to write of Vikings; of bloodshed and battles under the standard of the Raven ; on another of the saving of souls by men like Columba, Augustine, Paulinus, and Aidan. Here in England Christianity had become the great central fact of man's existence, and it was assailed by Odin, and Thor the god of Thunder. It will be part of our tale to show how the Christian Church saved Western civilization. It was a long fight, and before the battle was won Christianity was assailed from another quarter.

Mohammed was born about 570, and his followers conquered Egypt and Palestine 634-40, and Persia in 651. By 709 they had taken N. Africa from the Byzantine Empire, and Spain in 711 from the Visigoths. Their further inroads were not stopped until they were defeated by Charles Martel at Poitiers in 732. This was only the beginning of the long struggle between the Cross and Crescent, which was to culminate later in the Crusades. Enough has been written to show that when the Anglo-Saxons came to England, they were not moved to do so because they felt in need of a holiday, but were forced to it by the stress of circumstance. One point should be noted. In their early migrations they had come into contact with Gothic culture in S. Russia, and their love of colour and jewelry can be traced back to this source.

The Conquest of the Britons When the Roman legions left in 410, the Britons struggled against their enemies as best they could. Harried by the Picts from the North, they finally called to their assistance Hengest, a chief of the Anglo-Saxons. This was rather like trying to put out a fire by throwing petrol on it. Hengest came with his war band, to Ebbsfleet in Thanet, in 449, and repulsed the Picts, but by 457 he had conquered Kent on his own account. The glad news went across the North Sea, that here was a fat land where one could feel safe, so Hengest was followed by continually increasing swarms.

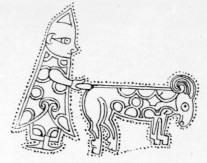

FIG. 8.—David rescuing the lamb from the lion. (Psalter, S. John's College, Cambridge.)

Go yourselves to Richborough, the old Roman fort guarding the port of Rutupiae, the door into England at the beginning of Watling Street. Look across the flats, which once were sea, to Ebbsfleet, and then imagine the hungry Saxons roving round Thanet ; spying out the land opposite and settling to conquer it.

Bede wrote : " From the Jutes are descended the people of Kent, and of the Isle of Wight, and those also in the province of the West Saxons who are to this day called Jutes, seated opposite the Isle of Wight. From the Saxons came the East Saxons, the South Saxons, and the West Saxons. From the Angles are descended the East Angles, the Middle Angles, Mercians, and all the race of the Northumbrians."

The period of conquest extended from 449, until the final defeat of the British by Egbert, King of Wessex, in 815. We have taken this as the first of the three chapters into which this book is divided. During this 366 years the Britons were being pushed continually into the West, that is for a period which, from our own time, would take us back to the days of Elizabeth's reign. The Legend of Arthur may rest on the doings of a British king, who resisted the Saxon invaders between 467-93. The Anglo-Saxon Chronicle, compiled in the time of Alfred, 891-2, should be consulted for the details of the invasion. As we do not wish to stain these pages too deeply in blood, we shall content ourselves with one quotation

7

FIG. 9.—Border. (Gospels of Durrow.)

from Bede, to show how desperate the struggle was. " Public as well as private structures were overturned ; the priests were everywhere slain before the altars ; the prelates and the people, without any respect of persons, were destroyed with fire and sword ; nor was there any to bury those who had been thus cruelly slaughtered. Some of the miserable remainder, being taken in the mountains, were butchered in heaps. Others, spent with hunger, came forth and submitted themselves to the enemy for food, being destined to undergo perpetual servitude, if they were not killed upon the spot."

This passage gives a far better idea than any words of ours, of what the impact of barbarism meant to the Romano-British civilization, and we are apt to forget the debt we may owe to the Britons to-day, in keeping Christianity alive in the West. In fact, we may not even think of them as Christians, until we remember that S. Alban was martyred as early as 304, here in England. S. Patrick went to Ireland about 427, before the coming of Hengest in 449, and it was the Irish Church which sent Columba to Iona about 563, and from Iona, Aidan went at a later date to Holy Isle, as we shall presently see. We must always remember that Great Britain was an outlier on the Roman Empire ; a North-West Province which was the outpost of its civilization, and by its island position cut off from Rome by the barbarian inroads. It may well be that the whole history of this country would have been different, if the Irish Church had not humanized life in the West, while the Anglo-Saxons were giving a very fair imitation of the Devil and all his works elsewhere.

Anglo-Saxon Characteristics

Before we trace the work of the Church in more detail, it may be well to go back and endeavour to find out if our Anglo-Saxon ancestors had any other qualities wherewith to qualify their ferocity.

Tacitus, who knew the breed, wrote: "They live apart, each by himself, as woodside, plain, or fresh spring attracts him" and this has remained a characteristic of Englishmen ever since; they have little civic pride, but love the country. Tacitus of course did not mean solitary men living by themselves, or even single families, as

FIG. 10.—Symbol of S. Mark.
(Gospels of Durrow.)

to-day, in ridiculous little houses in the suburbs. Even as late as the time of Sir Thomas More, we read that he built himself a house at Chelsea, where he lived with his wife, his son, and his daughter-in-law, his three daughters, and their husbands, with eleven grandchildren. In Anglo-Saxon times the families which lived together were even larger than this, and more like a tribe or clan. Bede always counts, not the number of inhabitants in a province, but tells you how many families it contained. As well he throws an interesting sidelight on family customs, he wrote of one "Orric, surnamed Oisc, from whom the kings of Kent are wont to be called Oiscings," and again "The son of Tytilus, whose father was Uuffa, from whom the kings of the East Angles are called Uuffings." If we turn to Bede again we find that the kings at first were what we should call chiefs, "for those Ancient Saxons have no king, but several lords that rule their nation; and when any war happens, they cast lots indifferently, and on whomsoever the lot falls, him they follow and obey during the war; but as soon as the war is ended, all those lords are again equal in power." When the Saxons came to England, we must think of these chiefs settling down, and calling their home Uuffing-ham, because it was the home of the Uuffings, who were the descendants of Uuffa.

From such simple beginnings our English villages have grown up. The chief built his Hall, and grouped around

C

it were the huts of his followers, and the bowers for the women-folk. The village had its Moot Hill, or places where Dooms or judgment was given, and a spring for water. The whole was girt round with a ditch and bank, with a palisaded fence on top. There were the common fields, and outside all, the Mark, where the stranger coming must blow his horn or risk death. The freeman was the freeholder of part of the land, and there cannot have been many slaves in the bands of warriors who came first, but later the Britons who were captured were enslaved, and as society became more settled, and the chieftains became kings, some men went up, and others sank into a servile class.

Domesday Book, completed in 1086, mentions parishes of the time of Edward the Confessor, which still remain, and which had their beginnings in the time we write of. The Hall of the chief became the Hall of the lord, and his Chapel, built when he became a Christian, developed into the Parish Church. Bede writes of an inn, and there would have been a mill for grinding corn. The system of farming was to remain as the general one until the enclosures in the eighteenth century gave it the death blow.

This is the outline on to which we have to graft fuller details, and our first step will be to familiarize ourselves with the appearance of the Anglo-Saxons, so that we may be able to fit them into the picture.

Clothes　　We may take it that the dress of the first Saxons who arrived here resembled that illustrated in Fig. 56, Part II ; this again was like that of the barbarians shown on the Trajan Column, and must have been common to the tribes, outside the Empire, across the Rhine and Danube. The Anglo-Saxon dress was a development of this.

In our plate, Fig. 11, the first figure on the left is a Thane. He wore a shirt, and breeches, sometimes to the ankles, and at others cut off at the knee, when hose like leggings were added, and fastened by cross garters which were part of the leather shoes. These latter were sometimes gilded. The breeches were probably fastened at the waist, by a belt passed through loops like cricketing trousers. Over the shirt, a wool, or linen, tunic reaching to the knee was worn. This was belted at the waist, and had long sleeves tight at the wrist, and fastened with metal clasps. The cloak was fastened

Fig. II. Anglo-Saxon Costume

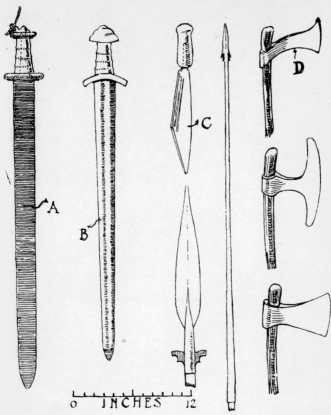

FIG. 12.—Saxon and Viking Arms.

on breast or shoulder with a brooch. For everyday use caps of Phrygian shape were worn.

The next man has much the same clothes, but is shown bearing arms. His tunic is a coat of mail formed of iron rings sewn on to the strong cloth. His helmet has an iron frame, filled in between with horn with a boar on the crest (see Beowulf page 20). The spear was the commonest weapon in the early pagan days; sometimes it had wings on it as Fig. 12, and the socket was formed by hammering the iron

11

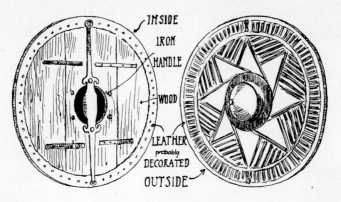

FIG. 13.—Anglo-Saxon Shield.

round until the sides met. The shaft of ash, 6 to 7 feet long, had an iron ferule. Some were thrown as javelins. The early swords were formidable weapons, a yard long, with a wooden scabbard (as A Fig. 12). The later types had a tapered blade, as B, Scramasaxes were sword-like knives, as C.

Battle-axes were used, and some were thrown, as D Fig. 12. Shields were of wood covered with hide, painted and gilded, sometimes oval, and at others round. Fig. 13 shows the hand-grip of one. The bow was not very much used.

The central figure in Fig. 11 shows how women were dressed. They had one linen undergarment, and a tunic to the feet. Sometimes there were two tunics girdled at the waist, the inner having long sleeves, and the outer shorter and wider ones. Over these came the mantle, hanging down at back and front, in a way which suggests a poncho pattern with central hole for the head. The brooches, which we discuss later, appear to have been worn in pairs. The head was covered with a silk or linen wrap. The women wore girdles, and girdle hangers like chatelaines have been found in their graves, and they had little bags.

They adorned themselves with fine barbaric necklaces; big lumps of amber, crystal, amethyst, or beads of glass coloured in many ways. One in the British Museum has beads made of gold wire coiled to a barrel-like shape, with

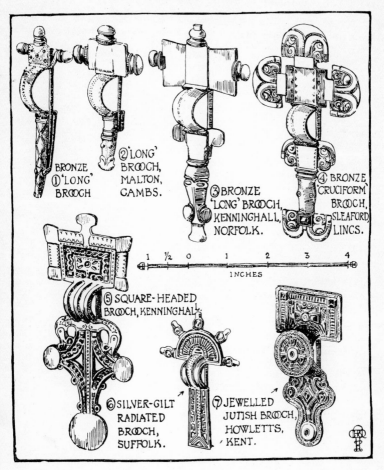

① BRONZE 'LONG' BROOCH

② 'LONG' BROOCH, MALTON, CAMBS.

③ BRONZE 'LONG' BROOCH, KENNINGHALL, NORFOLK.

④ BRONZE 'CRUCIFORM' BROOCH, SLEAFORD, LINCS.

1 ½ 0 1 2 3 4

INCHES

⑤ SQUARE-HEADED BROOCH, KENNINGHALL.

⑥ SILVER-GILT RADIATED BROOCH, SUFFOLK.

⑦ JEWELLED JUTISH BROOCH, HOWLETTS, KENT.

FIG. 14.—Anglo-Saxon Brooches.

garnet pendants hanging between. Sometimes these were worn festooned across the chest, or as bracelets.

We cannot illustrate all the beautiful things which were used. Belts had jewelled buckles, and there were armlets, and rings. Pins of all patterns were made ; Ireland was the home of what are called hand-pins, with the head cranked like a modern tie-pin. The horse was trapped out as beautifully as his master. Children's dress was a miniature edition of that of their parents.

The ceorl on the right of Fig. 11, would have worn the same type of clothes as his master, but everything would have been simpler and rougher. He carried no sword. This was the weapon of the earl or Thane.

Brooches   This will be a good place in which to show the development of the brooches which were used to fasten the cloaks. These can be traced back to S. Russia, where they were used by the Goths, before they migrated to E. Prussia, and from the Baltic Coast to Scandinavia. Fig. 14 has been drawn to show some of the developments of the brooch. 1, probably East Anglian, is perhaps as early as the fifth century, and the same pattern, with the horse-like head on the foot, is found as well in Sweden. All these brooches are glorified versions of our old friend the safety-pin, but with a spring on both sides of the head, see 5, Fig. 77, Part II which shows the beginnings in the Bronze and Early Iron Ages.

2, Fig. 14, shows the next development. The knobs on the bar are now cast in one piece with the brooch. This type dates from the end of the fifth century. 3 shows a further and later development. 4 illustrates why this type is called " cruciform " ; it dates from the seventh century, and is a beautiful piece, with small silver panels on the arms of the cross, and garnet inlay on the nostrils of the horse. 5 is a square-headed brooch which resembles types started in Denmark ; this is earlier than 4, dating from about 500. 6 is a radiated brooch, of which parallels have been found in the Crimea ; this is a fifth century type. 7 has its own peculiar Jutish design.

The Anglo-Saxons used as well circular brooches, sometimes made as a solid disc, and at others as an embossed plate cemented on to a disc with vertical edge, the pin at the back being hinged.

The jewelled circular brooches found in Kent are extraordinarily fine. Some are like the disc applied to the bow of 7, Fig. 14. This is called the keystone brooch, because the garnet inlays are mounted in the form of wedges, like the keystones of an arch ; the central boss being of ivory, or some similar white substance. Others are far more elaborately decorated with garnets, and blue glass to imitate lapis lazuli, and gold filigree work applied to the background. The Kentish jewelry has parallels in the Rhineland and Italy, and its best period is about 600.

There are quoit brooches, so called because of their shape, made of silver, partly gilt. There were wonderful developments of the penannular types shaped like an incomplete ring and noted in the Early Iron Age, Part II, page 95, in Anglo-Saxon times, some having pins 2 feet long.

Fine jewelry needs good material to show it off, and there is evidence that the Anglo-Saxon women were expert weavers. Gold threads have been found in graves, generally in a position which suggests that they were originally woven into a head-dress. This may have been produced in the same way as the ephod made for Aaron, " they did beat the gold into thin plates, and cut it into wires, to work it in the blue, and in the purple, and in the scarlet, and in the fine linen, with cunning work."

This joyous use of colour was not confined to costume, but was common to everything. It was something which men brought with them from the East, and one wishes that it could come our way again. Women to-day have a gay colour sense, but men, alas, with the exception of under-graduates and golfers, since that dismal revolution which is called " Industrial," have become greyer and sadder every year.

The materials of which we have been writing were of *Weaving* course woven on a loom, and drawings in the manuscripts suggest that this had been developed. As we last saw it in Fig. 53, Part II, the warp was stretched by warp weights ; now a bottom roller was added, which got rid of the weights, and enabled a greater length of material to be made. Iron blades, like short two-edged swords, have been found in women's graves, and these are thought to have been used to pack the weft threads together on to those of the warp. The weaving was done as described on page 62, Part II.

Perhaps one of the most interesting exhibits in any Museum is the work-box, as Fig. 15, which was found in a grave, and is now in the B.M. It was gilded and belonged to an Anglo-

Saxon mother whom we will name, Aelswitha, and her husband was Aethulf, and they had, as they did in those days, a large family, and there was one boy, Aelfred, the hero of this short tale, and his mother said to him, " Aelfred, I cannot imagine what you do to wear out your *brecs* so quickly, these were new only last week, and now, look at the holes ; " and Aelfred did not find anything to say. The End. We know all this, because the work-box contained thread, wool, linen and needles.

Writing of boys, reminds us that King Alfred made his Grandson Athelstan, " a knight unusually early, giving him a scarlet cloak, a belt studded with diamonds, and a Saxon sword with a golden scabbard." Think of the colour of a crowd of Athelstans.

Ecclesias-
tical
Dress

Here we may give a note on ecclesiastical costumes. In the priest's vestments the long white tunic became the alb. The upper tunic with looser and shorter sleeves, the dalmatic. The mantle developed into the chasuble, and its hood became the cope.

There is also the traditional costume in which Our Lord and the Saints, and Angels, are always shown. First comes a long sleeved tunic, then there is a mantle, one end of which hangs down from the left shoulder in front, the remainder being taken behind the back, and passed under the right shoulder and across the front to be draped over the left arm or shoulder. This dress is much in the classical fashion of the Roman toga described on page 40, Part III.

Saxon
England

Having obtained some idea of the appearance of the Saxons, we must search for the local colour of their background, and we cannot do better than study Bede's History. Its date, about 730, makes it very important. The final conquest of the Britons, in 815, was approaching ; the Danes had not yet appeared to plunder and destroy, so the picture given by Bede, is of the apex of Anglo-Saxon civilization.

He opens with a description, " Britain, an island in the ocean, formerly called Albion . . . excels for grain and trees, and is well adapted for feeding cattle and beasts of burden. It also produces vines in some places, and has plenty of land and water-fowls of several sorts ; it is remarkable also for rivers abounding in fish, and plentiful springs. It has the greatest plenty of salmon and eels ; seals are frequently

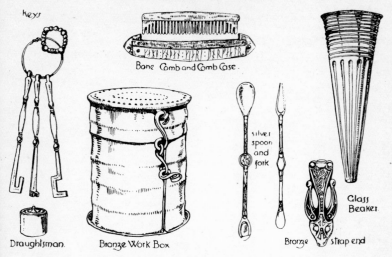

Keys

Bone Comb and Comb Case.

silver spoon and fork

Glass Beaker.

Draughtsman.

Bronze Work Box

Bronze strap end

FIG. 15.—Anglo-Saxon Knick-knacks.

taken, and dolphins, as also whales; besides many sorts of shell-fish, such as mussels, in which are often found excellent pearls of all colours, red, purple, violet, and green, but mostly white. There is also a great abundance of cockles, of which the scarlet dye is made; a most beautiful colour which never fades with the heat of the sun or the washing of the rain; but the older it is the more beautiful it becomes. It has both salt and hot springs, and from them flow rivers which furnish hot baths proper for all ages and sexes, and arranged according."

This sounds as if by 730 the hot springs at Bath had been rediscovered.

Bede mentions copper, iron, lead, silver and jet, "which is black and sparkling, glittering at the fire, and when heated drives away serpents; being warmed with rubbing, it holds fast whatever is applied to it, like amber." He goes on to say, "this island at present, contains five nations, the English, Britons, Scots (meaning the Irish), Picts, and Latins (Romanized Britons), each in its own peculiar dialect cultivating the sublime study of Divine truth. The Latin tongue

17

D

is, by the study of the Scriptures, become common to all the rest.''

Even in Bede's time, the people do not appear to have been town dwellers, because he writes, '' The island was *formerly* embellished with twenty-eight noble cities, besides innumerable castles, which were all strongly secured with walls, towers, gates and locks.'' Some of the Roman towns though were being used, because we read in 604, '' The East Saxons, who are divided from Kent by the river Thames, and border on the Eastern sea. Their metropolis is the city of London, which is situated on the bank of the aforesaid river, and is the mart of many nations resorting to it by sea and land.''

We do not know how far the Roman Londinium had been destroyed, but there must have been considerable remains to influence the Saxon builders. Perhaps they patched them up here and there, and added timber buildings when new ones were necessary. Abbot Biscop, who built the monastery at Jarrow, where Bede lived, is said to have been '' the first person who introduced in England constructors of stone edifices, as well as the makers of glass windows,'' meaning of course the first after the Romans.

In 710, the king of the Picts wrote to Abbot Ceolfrid, of Jarrow, to send him architects '' to build a church in his nation after the Roman manner.'' Mellitus, bishop of the East Saxons, built the church of S. Paul in the city of London, and this may have been in the Roman manner. We discuss this again in King Alfred's time.

Saxon Houses We will now consider the Hall of the Chief. This was to remain, until the days of Elizabeth, as the central feature of the house in which all the household met for meals and jollity. Even to-day, the big house in a village is very often called the Hall. The bowers, and kitchens, which at first were separate buildings, were gradually tacked on to the body of the Hall, until in the fourteenth and fifteenth centuries they all come under the same roof, and the modern house takes shape.

Beowulf If we turn to Beowulf, the great Anglo-Saxon poem, we find the early type of Hall described, and there are many interesting details of everyday life. Also please note that people really did believe in dragons in those days.

Fig. 16.—Imaginary reconstruction of Anglo-Saxon Homestead.

ANGLO-SAXON ENGLAND

The only manuscript of Beowulf is in the British Museum. This dates from about 1000, but deals with life about 550. The poem opens with an account of the passing of Scyld, the Warrior King, who lived in earlier days and gave the Danes their name of Scyldings. Scyld was carried down to his ship, and placed by the mast ; the dead eyes looking ahead. Weapons and treasure were put aboard, and his standard high above his head, the ship was pushed out on the flood, to sail into the unknown seas beyond the horizon. Then we read of Beowulf : Beowulf was a prince of the Geatas, of the Baltic island of Gotland. He went to Denmark, to visit Hrothgar, who had built a Mead Hall, named Heorot, as a habitation for his retainers. This hall was lofty and wide gabled, and gold-bespangled, the door fastened by forged bands. These were not sufficient to keep out the fiend Grendel, who came at night and carried off the warriors sleeping after the banquet. Men sought beds among the outbuildings to escape.

Then came Beowulf in his fresh tarred ship, over the swan's road. With him were fourteen champions, above whose cheek-guards shone the boar-images covered with gold. Their corslets were hard, hand-locked, and glistened, each gleaming ring of iron chinked in their harness. Landing in Denmark, they travelled by a paved road, and arrived at Heorot. Here they put their shields against the wall, and sat themselves on the benches.

Hrothgar was not in the Hall. He had a Chamber close by where he sat with his nobles. Beowulf went there, by a path between, and explained his mission, and was after entertained at a banquet in the Hall. Wealhtheow, the queen, entered and bore the mead cup to Beowulf. He and his men slept in the Hall, and there came Grendel, and killed one man. The monster was attacked by Beowulf, but escaped, with the loss of an arm, only to die later in the mere where he lived.

Again there was a banquet, and the Hall was decorated with gold embroidered tapestries. The song was sung, the gleeman's lay. Then mirth rose high, the noise of revelry was clearly heard ; cup-bearers proferred wine from curious vessels. After the men slept in the Hall. '' They cleared the bench-boards, it was spread about with beds and bolsters.

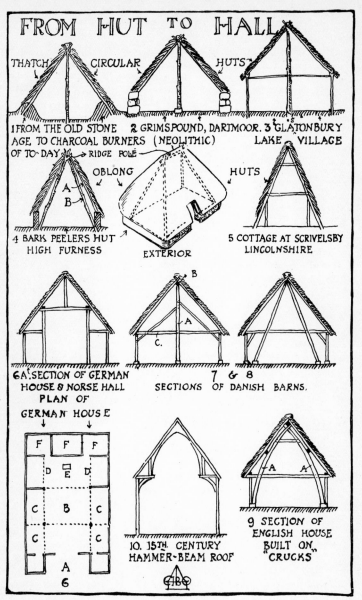

FROM HUT TO HALL

THATCH   CIRCULAR   HUTS

1 FROM THE OLD STONE AGE TO CHARCOAL BURNERS OF TO-DAY   2 GRIMSPOUND, DARTMOOR. (NEOLITHIC)   3 GLASTONBURY LAKE VILLAGE

RIDGE POLE

OBLONG   HUTS

A
B

4 BARK PEELERS HUT HIGH FURNESS

EXTERIOR

5 COTTAGE AT SCRIVELSBY LINCOLNSHIRE

B
A
C.

6 A. SECTION OF GERMAN HOUSE & NORSE HALL   7 & 8 SECTIONS OF DANISH BARNS.

PLAN OF GERMAN HOUSE

F   F   F
D   E   D
C   B   C
C   C
A
6

10. 15TH CENTURY HAMMER-BEAM ROOF

A   A

9 SECTION OF ENGLISH HOUSE BUILT ON "CRUCKS"

FIG. 17.—Development of Roofs.

They set war-bucklers at their heads, the shining shield-wood. There on the bench, above each noble, was exposed the helmet, prominent in war, the ringed mail-coat, the proud spear-shaft. It was ever their practice to be ready for the fray at home or in the field."

But Grendel's mother came to avenge his death, and carried off a noble. Beowulf was not in the Hall, having had a separate lodging assigned to him as a special honour. He went to the King's Bower, and then led a band on horseback, who traced the steps of the monster to the mere. Here Beowulf put on his armour and went down into the lake, and swimming to the bottom, found there a cavern where no water harmed him in any way. Here was fought the fight with the she-wolf of the deep. His own sword failed him, but in the cavern he found an old titanic sword, and with it gained the victory, and having killed the mother, cut the head off the dead body of Grendel.

The watchers on the bank viewed the blood-stained waters with gloomy foreboding, and the disheartened Danes went home. Later Beowulf swam up with Grendel's head and found his own men waiting. They returned to Heorot, where once again there was great rejoicing, and Hrothgar made a fine speech congratulating Beowulf, but warned him, that though God deals out to mankind many gifts, the soul's guardian may sleep, and man wax insolent, and arrogant, and so be " struck at the heart under his armour, by the piercing arrow—-the crooked strange behests of the malignant spirit."

Beowulf returned to the land of the Geats, and told his king, Hygelac, of his adventures, seated opposite to him in the Hall. Later he became king himself, and ruled well until his own land was oppressed by a dragon, 50 feet long, winged, and vomiting fire. The monster lived in a barrow, " the primeval earth-dwelling contained within it rocky arches," and guarded there a hoard of treasure. A drinking bowl was stolen by a thrall, and the dragon ravaged the countryside in revenge. Then Beowulf, now an old man, girded on his armour for his last fight, and killing the dragon, was himself killed by it.

His funeral pyre was made on the cliff by the sea, and around it were hung helmets, shields, and corslets, and then

Fig. 18.—Barn, Widdington, N.W. Essex.

Beowulf was laid in its midst. When his body was consumed by fire, they heaped up a barrow on the remains, and in it placed the treasure of the dragon, "where it still exists, as unprofitable to men as it had been before."

The poem is of extraordinary interest, because it gives the outlook on life of the ordinary man. With Bede we see the world through a monk's eyes, but in Beowulf we have the thoughts of the warrior. It must have been sung by poets in a thousand Halls until some Saxon Homer set it out in proper form.

There are many details in the poem, which suggest that the Halls Hall of Heorot was a timber-framed building, rather like a

23

glorified barn. We have attempted a reconstruction of the exterior in Fig. 16, and of the interior in Fig. 1.

One important detail of these early Halls should be noted, the principal seat instead of being on a raised dais at the end, as it was in the later mediaeval Halls, was placed in the centre of the north side. The chief guest had his seat opposite on the south side, and here was a window. Women sat on cross benches at the end. The fire was placed centrally.

Bede recounts how a traveller came to a village and entered a house where the neighbours were feasting. " They sat long at supper and drank hard, with a great fire in the middle of the room ; it happened that the sparks flew up and caught the top of the house, which being made of wattles and thatch, was presently in a flame."

We see in Beowulf how there were sleeping rooms in other buildings. In one saga we find that these were on the first floor, reached by an outer staircase, because a guest, going up to bed, opened the wrong door and fell into the mead vat under instead.

Timber Framing Timber framing has remained very characteristic of English building. The average Englishman is frequently quite a handy man with saw and chisel, and can frame up a respectable hut or barn, and wherever he goes he carries with him this timber building tradition which he has inherited from his Anglo-Saxon forefathers. Modern building bye-laws repress his instincts here in England, but in the Dominions, and the United States of America, the trail of the Anglo-Saxon is marked by timber building.

Tacitus, writing in the first century A.D., said that " none of the Germanic peoples dwell in cities, and they do not even tolerate houses which are built in rows. They dwell apart, and at a distance from one another, according to the preference which they may have for the stream, the plain, or the grove. . . . They do not make use of stone cut from the quarry, or of tiles ; for every kind of building they make use of unshapely wood, which falls short of beauty or attractiveness. They carefully colour some parts of their buildings with earth which is so clear and bright as to resemble painting and coloured designs."

German Houses Archaeologists interested in the design of houses have searched in Germany, around the Elbe, and Weser, from

THE ROD, POLE OR PERCH

Fig. 19.—Original Hall, Stanton's Farm, Black Notley, near Braintree, Essex.

where the Anglo-Saxons came, for surviving types of timber-framed buildings. This was quite a proper thing to do, because a thousand years is nothing in the development of the design of a house. Until the Enclosures, in the eighteenth century, and the Industrial Revolution in the nineteenth, country life had not altered in its essentials very much from that of the times of the Anglo-Saxons. A house built in the sixteenth century and surviving to-day, especially if it is obviously akin to another built in the fourteenth, which again is the descendant of still earlier types, may be very useful in tracing the evolution of the English house.

Fig. 17 (6) shows a typical plan of one of these German houses, dating from about the sixteenth century, which in its general form resembles a barn. A large pair of doors at A, open into a space like the nave of a church at B, with aisles at the sides at C. Horses were stabled in one aisle, and cows in the other, with their heads towards the central space from which they were fed. The hay and corn were kept in the roof space over. The men servants slept over one aisle, and the women over the other. The farmer lived in the space D D, which resembled the transepts of a church, and here was the fire, E, the smoke from which wafted through the building, and helped to keep down the smell of the cattle. The rooms at F F were additions for the comfort of the family. 6A shows the section of the building, and the old Norse Hall is supposed to have followed the same lines.

If our readers will now turn to Fig. 18 of the Essex Barn, they will notice how closely its construction follows that of the German house Fig. 17, 6A, and again Fig. 19 of the timber-framed aisled Hall in Essex is obviously in the same tradition. We do not suggest that cattle were ever stabled in the Essex Hall, but Mr. Addy, in his book, gives very interesting examples of Yorkshire farms where this practice was followed, and in Ireland, the pig, by reason of being the gentleman who paid the rent, lived with the family.

The Essex Hall, Fig. 19, is still in use as a farmhouse, though much altered and added to. Originally it consisted of the Hall, with perhaps only a kitchen and Bower as additions. The rafters of the roof are still covered with the soot from the smoke which came up from the fire on the floor under.

Fig. 17 (7 and 8) show sections of barns in Jutland, Denmark. 7 has a row of posts, A, supporting the ridge pole B. Here we see why we talk about the king post in roofs to-day, because in the old days they were the Kings of the Posts ; but they must have been inconvenient, because later we find that the king post was made to stand on the tie-beam, C, so named because it tied in the walls. This is shown in 6A, where the main part of the building has been raised and side aisles added. Fig. 17 (8) shows another Danish roof truss. Here instead of the inconvenient centre king post, a pair of posts are straddled across the barn to carry the ridge pole.

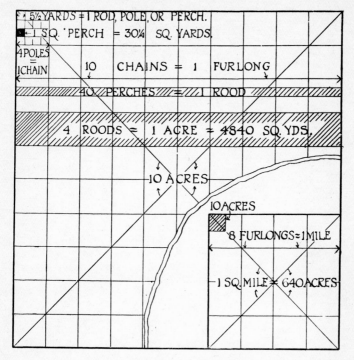

FIG. 20.—Rod as Unit of Land Measurement.

If we now turn to Fig. 17 (9), we find a method of roofing which at one time was very common in the N. and Midlands of England. A curved trunk of an oak was selected and sawn in half, the two pieces, called crucks or crooks, being set up, with the tops crossed to carry the ridge pole, and a tie-beam to prevent the walls spreading. It looks as if 8 and 9 can claim affinity, and ideas being the scarcest things in the world, we have here not two ideas of building, but only one.

The problem of how to keep a roof over his head is one that has always worried man, so we have collected together the earlier types already illustrated in our books.

Fig. 17 (1) shows the most primitive form of human habitation. Its form is suggested in a la Madaleine drawing of the Old Stone Age, see Part I, page 91, and it is still used by charcoal burners. In the New Stone, and Bronze Ages, we find that walls have been added as 2, and shown in more detail in Fig. 19, Part II. By the Early Iron Age the walls have raised themselves up, and the form is 3 of the Glastonbury Lake Village, shown in Fig. 68, Part II. Now we come to an interesting development, when the circular plan was given up for an oblong form. (4) Fig. 17, of a bark peeler's hut in High Furness, gives us an idea of how the change may have been effected. Here two pairs of poles, having their feet on an oblong of 13 feet by 8, are inclined together to support a ridge pole, 4 feet long. Low wattle walls support the rafters at A, which carry the thatch. The pairs of poles, at B, have not yet taken the upright position of those in 8, and it looks as if this type of building began by cutting a circular hut in half and adding the short ridge pole in the middle ; however that may be, there is an obvious connection between 4 and 8, Fig. 17. 5 shows the section of an amusing house we saw some years ago at Scrivelsby, Lincolnshire, known as Teapot Hall, where the rafters are taken down into the ground without any vertical external walls. 10 shows how the later hammer-beam roofs of the fifteenth century developed out of 6A by omitting the posts to the aisles.

We have given these details. so that our readers may see how we went to work in our reconstructions of Anglo-Saxon timber buildings.

Mensuration

Mensuration is a subject well worth studying. The Saxon builder, building a Hall, or the steward settling a question of land, had to employ a unit of measurement that everybody understood.

In Part III, page 18, we wrote of Roman measurement, and the normal Roman foot was 296 m/m., or a full $11\frac{5}{8}$ English inches. The unit of Roman land measurement was the Iugerum, or 240 feet by 120. To-day we measure land by the acre, which is one furlong, or furrow-long, in length, by one chain in breadth, see Fig. 20. This arose from the practice in the Middle Ages of marking off the Common Fields in strips, which were a furrow long, and were measured for breadth by a chain. Boys and girls may be worried, when they

URN ABOUT
8½" DIAM.

FIG. 21.—Urn with implements found in it. (British Museum.)

find that in the old days, the acres, and the rods, poles, or perches varied in different parts of the country. There is an explanation for this.

To-day, weights, and measures, are fixed by a standard which is settled by Government, and these are uniform throughout the country ; but this was not possible in the old days. This is how they managed it in the sixteenth century : " Stand at the door of a church on a Sunday, and bid sixteen men to stop, tall ones and small ones, as they happen to pass out when the service is finished ; then make them put their left feet one behind the other, and the length thus obtained shall be a right and lawful rod to measure and survey the land with, and the sixteenth part of it shall be a right and lawful foot." We can see that in this way the rod would vary and that it paid to have large feet. We must think of this rod as the unit, and not worry about its equivalent in feet and inches to-day.

Mr. Addy thinks the rod came about because it was the space which four of the oxen used for ploughing needed for standing room in the stalls of their stable, and if we test the plans of old houses, churches, and even cathedrals, we find that they seem to have been set out with a rod. In old

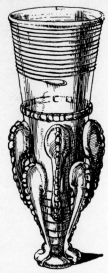

FIG. 22.—Anglo-
Saxon Glass.
(British Museum.)

documents, buildings are described as consisting of so many bays.

It would be quite an interesting thing, to find out the length of the old rod in one's own county, and then test it on the bays of the church, and any other old buildings. Mensuration may not sound a very interesting subject, but let us take the Hall shown in Fig. 19, and imagine the carpenter arriving on the scene to discuss its erection. He meets the man who wants to build, and with his rod, which he is shown holding upright, proceeds to peg out on the ground the plan of the Hall. When the carpenter said, " Your Hall will be two rods wide, with aisles at the side, which will be half a rod in width, and you can have it two, or three bays, each of a rod in length," he was talking in terms which the owner understood.

Having dealt with the Hall, and
Household how it was built, we may as well discuss the table furniture
Gear of the Anglo-Saxons. Our drawing, Fig. 1, shows a banquet in progress. Each man carried his own knife. Fig. 21 shows one of these, from a burial, where it had been placed for the use of its owner in the spirit world. Fig. 15 shows a silver fork and spoon, found in a hoard at Sevington, Wilts, of about 880 ; the fork is remarkable because "fingers were made before forks" was the rule until late in the Middle Ages.

The table glass was very beautiful ; not a clear white, but in ambers, blues, and greens, decorated in a very glass-blowing way with tears, or gouts, as Fig. 22, of the molten metal, which being hollow inside, are in some miraculous way connected with the inside so that the wine could flow into them. Others have spidery threads laid on. In A. S. times, the tumblers did tumble, because they had no foot to stand on, and the contents had to be tossed off at a draught. Fig. 15

Fig. 23.—Anglo-Saxon Glass. (British Museum.)

shows one of these. Other patterns are shown in Figs. 22, 23 and 24.

Pottery of course was made, and Figs. 21 and 25 show cinerary urns. Fig. 26 shows a rare jug from the British Museum, dating from the fifth century. Its handle is perforated as a spout. Fig. 27 shows a bottle of reddish ware. This is Jutish, and the Jutes' pottery, like their jewelry, was different from that of the Angles and Saxons. Fig. 28 is a Saxon cup.

The houses were lighted by candles. William of Malmesbury tells how when Ethelred II was a boy of 10 years old, " he so irritated his furious mother by his weeping, that not having a whip at hand, she beat the little innocent with some candles she had snatched up . . . . on this account he dreaded candles during the rest of his life."

When we turn to the personal belongings of the Anglo- Burial Saxons, we shall have to study these in connection with their burials. This may sound a little dismal, but all the everyday things we possess of the period have been found in graves. With one exception, at Sutton Courtney, which is not very helpful, there is no site which can be instanced as Anglo-Saxon, as in Silchester and Roman Britain, with which we dealt in Part III.

Graves however are a wonderful indication of the outlook of a people. The heathen sometimes burned his dead, and buried with the ashes, arms, and implements, for use in the

Fig. 24.—Anglo-Saxon Glass. (British Museum.)

spirit world. In doing this, he was more helpful to the archaeologist than the Christian, who was buried, to await the Resurrection, without any such aids.

In Parts I to III, we have traced how the changes were rung through the centuries, between burial by burning, cremation, and by interring the unburned body in the earth, called inhumation. At the end of the Roman period inhumation became general. This was altered once more, because the Saxons burned their dead. Fig. 25 shows one of their cinerary urns from the British Museum. These are grey, brown, or black, and what is very extraordinary, they are not turned on a wheel, but are hand-made, like the pre-historic pottery described on page 25, Part II. Cremation seems to have appealed very especially to the Anglians, and was retained longer by them than by the Saxons. The Jutes always favoured inhumation.

Fig. 21 shows a cinerary urn from the British Museum, with the implements which were buried with the ashes. Smaller pots perhaps contained food and drink for use on the journey to the other world. In Case 50, at the British Museum, can be seen the contents of the grave of a chieftain at Taplow. This was dug 12 feet long, by 8 feet wide, by 6 feet deep, and E. and W., but the head was at the E., instead of at the W., as in Christian usage. The spear lay inverted at the side of the skeleton and the sword was placed ready to hand. The gold buckle, and clasps of the belt, are very beautiful, set with garnets, and lapis-lazuli. Above the head were two shields, an iron knife and ring. To the S.E. was a bucket, and bronze bowl. There were glass cups, and the remains of a large tub which had been placed over the thighs of the warrior. Two drinking horns as Fig. 29 were there to quench his thirst, and what is rather touching, 30 bone draughtsmen accompanied him to while away the time. There is another set at the British Museum made from horses' teeth.

The grave at Taplow was covered with a barrow or mound of earth, and its furniture gives us a very good idea of the belongings of a chieftain. Heathen burials ceased with the final conversion of the English by Wilfrid about 681.

Tombstones were used in later Saxon times. There is a bronze model of one at the British Museum, and fragments of others, and of a memorial cross with a runic inscription imploring prayers for Cynibalth Cuthbertson. The Museum has examples of small slabs, known as pillow stones, on which crosses are carved, and which were placed under the heads of the bodies.

Having been driven to Death by our subject, we turn now to the saving of Life.

The practice of medicine in Anglo-Saxon times, seems to have consisted of Faith Healing, assisted by rough surgery. In 660, the physician Cynefrid operated on Queen Etheldrida, who had " a very great swelling under her jaw." " And I was ordered," said he, " to lay open that swelling, to let out the noxious matter in it." **Medicine**

Again in 698, the surgeons were puzzled by a youth whose eyelid had a great swelling on it. They " applied their medicines to ripen it, but in vain. Some said it ought to be cut off ; others opposed it, for fear of worse consequences."

Another sad case was that of a virgin, who laboured under a grievous distemper, and was bled in the arm. A bishop was asked to help, but said, " You did very indiscreetly and unskilfully to bleed her in the fourth day of the moon ; for I remember that Archbishop Theodore, of blessed memory, said that bleeding at that time was very dangerous, when the light of the moon and the tide of the ocean is increasing ; and what can I do to the girl if she is like to die ? "

Matters were not arranged very cheerfully for the patients. An earl's servant had lost the use of all his limbs, and again a bishop was called in and " saw him in a dying condition, and the coffin at his side."

Bede writes, " a sudden pestilence (664) also depopulated the southern coasts of Britain, and afterwards extending into the province of the Northumbrians, ravaged the country far and near, and destroyed a great multitude of men." These plagues recurred through the centuries, and were caused by the dirty habits of people, and the fouling of water supply. The jointed drain pipes of Mycenae, and the uses of the sewers of Roman Britain were forgotten. The quotation from Bede, given on page 17, suggests that by his time the hot springs at Bath were again being used, but how far baths formed part of the plan of a house in Saxon times, as they did in those of the Romanised Britons, cannot be said. Even to-day we have hardly caught the latter up in the way of bathing.

The Church in Saxon times introduced the very bad practice of burying within the sacred building. Bede wrote of another which the doctors of to-day would hardly recommend. S. Chad was buried and " the place of the sepulchre is a wooden monument, made like a little house, covered, having a hole in the wall, through which those that go thither for devotion usually put in their hand and take out some of the dust, which they put into water and give to sick cattle or men to drink, upon which they are presently eased of their infirmity, and restored to health."

Education However, we shall have a totally wrong idea of the Anglo-Saxons, if we think of them as ignorant barbarians. At the end of our first period, in 781, before the Danes had wasted the country, Alcuin, a Northumbrian educated at York, went to the Court of Charlemagne and gave him a thorough knowledge of logic, rhetoric, and astronomy. This is a feather in the cap of the Anglo-Saxons, that the man who was governing all Western Europe, with the exception of Spain, should have turned to them for instruction.

Bede tells us that as early as 635, King Sigebert " being desirous to imitate the good institutions which he had seen in France, he set up a school for youth (at Seaham or Dunwich) to be instructed in literature." Theodore (669) assisted by Hadrian " gathered a crowd of disciples . . . and, together with the books of holy writ, they also taught them the arts of ecclesiastical poetry, astronomy, and arithmetic. A testimony of which is, that there are still living at this day some of their scholars, who are as well versed in the Greek and Latin tongues as in their own."

Fig. 25.—Burial Urn.
(British Museum.)

Children started their schooling at an early age. Bede wrote of a boy, Esica, not above three years old, placed in a monastery to pursue his studies. In these days of School Boards, we are apt to forget how large a share the Church has had in Education. For many centuries the actual church was the school-house. Evelyn, born 1620, tells us in his Diary : " I was not initiated into any rudiments till nearly five years of age, and then one Frier taught us at the church-porch of Wotton."

We do not hear much about games in Saxon times, perhaps, because life was so interesting that it was more amusing to play at being grown up, with romps in between, as the Eskimo children do to-day. They have small weapons and implements and learn their job by playing at it. Small Saxon battle-axes have been found which suggest this. Here is a note on horse racing. " We came into a plain and open road, well adapted for galloping our horses. The young men that were with him, and particularly those of the laity, began to entreat the bishop to give them leave to gallop, and make trial of the goodness of their horses."

Bede was not only the first of the English historians, but a classical scholar as well. He referred to Plato's " Republic " when he wrote : " a certain worldly writer most truly said, that the world would be most happy if either kings were philosophers, or philosophers were kings."

It was in a monastery at Whitby, that Caedmon, one of

Literature

35

the lay brothers, first received inspiration, and became the father of English poetry.

Gildas, who has been called the British Jeremiah, wrote his history as early as 545. It might have been of supreme interest, but unfortunately for us, the book, starting as a history, very speedily develops into a moral lecture. Gildas has hardly a good word to say for the Britons, who were delivered into the hands of the Saxons because of their sins ; then the turn of the Saxons comes, and they are denounced as being " a race hateful both to God and man." Gildas has one interesting reference to the " diabolical idols . . . of which we still see some mouldering away within or without the deserted temples, with stiff and deformed features as was customary." As he refers also to walled towns, these architectural remains must have been survivals of Romano-British building.

Giants   Geoffrey of Monmouth lived much later, between 1100-54. He must have been a delightful person. One phrase gives a taste of his quality : " The island was then called Albion and was inhabited by none but a few giants." As we have not yet interested ourselves in the everyday life of giants we have not drawn on Geoffrey for information. He wrote, or, as he himself says, translated into Latin, a very ancient book of British History. He did this because neither Gildas nor Bede said anything " of those kings who lived here before the Incarnation of Christ, nor of Arthur." Bede probably doubted the authenticity of their figures, and we suspect that the " ancient book " existed only in Geoffrey's imagination. What he did, was to gather all the legends together, to serve the very useful purpose of being the fountain head from which the poets and writers of romance drew their inspiration. There are happenings in Greece and Rome, and Gaul and Britain. Leir and Cordeilla, Merlin and the magicians and Arthur all live in his pages.

We must now consider Manuscripts, because these writings on vellum were the means by which the literature of the time was given to the people. An idea to-day can be radiated around the world at the speed of Light. In Anglo-Saxon times it had to be written and then carried by hand.

In the history of the subject, which extends from the Egyptian papyri of the fifteenth century B.C., to the time of printing by Caxton in the fifteenth century A.D., it is noteworthy that two of the greatest masterpieces in manuscripts were produced in the British Isles : the Lindisfarne Gospels, and the Book of Kells ; see Figs. 30 and 31.

The Romans used manuscripts, as everyone had to do before the days of printing, and when these were illuminated, the drawings remind one of the wall paintings of Pompeii. In 330, when the imperial government moved from Rome to

Manuscripts

FIG. 26.—Anglo-Saxon Jug.
(British Museum.)

Constantinople, their art took on that flavour which we call Byzantine, and the figures in the illuminations were like the mosaics at Ravenna.

Illuminating was started in the Irish monasteries at the end of the fifth century, and in all probability was introduced by S. Patrick when he went there in 437 from Rome. However that may be, a wonderful school of artists arose in Ireland, who produced work of the greatest beauty, and originality. They depended very largely on pattern into which animal forms were introduced ; these were purposely lengthened, and turned, and twisted, in the most amazing fashion, and are called lacertine. The human figures are more symbolic than realistic. Their masterpiece, the Book of Kells, dates from the eighth or early ninth century ; see Fig. 30.

From Ireland the art spread to England, and the Lindisfarne Gospels, or Durham Book, is Irish-Saxon in character. The ornament is Irish, but the figure drawing is realistic, and influenced by Byzantine work (Fig. 31). It must be remembered that the books were produced in the Scriptorium of the monastery, and many of the monks would have been employed in this way in the production of what was part of their missionary enterprise. Then perhaps a bishop would come from Rome, and bring with him a book illuminated in a novel way, and show it to the monks, who we may be sure would not be slow to adopt the new idea.

Probably Augustine brought books with him, because a classical influence is evident in illumination after his time.

In the ninth and tenth centuries we begin to get outline drawings which can be regarded as the forerunners of modern book illustrations. The Utrecht Psalter has many drawings which in their own quaint way are full of life and movement. Many of these have been used to illustrate English history books ; there is the amusing one of six gentlemen who appear to be combining physical culture with playing an organ. Unfortunately, now, it has been discovered that the Psalter is not Anglo-Saxon, but was done in N.E. France.

This work led up to that of the Winchester School. King Edgar's Foundation Charter, granted to the New Minster at Winchester, 966, continues the outline drawing, with stiff conventional borders derived from classical, and not Celtic sources. The Liber Vitae of Newminster has beautiful outline drawing and portraits of Canute and his queen. By the eleventh century we have the Grimbald Gospels, done at Winchester, in which the figure subjects, drawn in outline, are surrounded by panelled frames of figures on which are imposed circular medallions giving great richness.

We strongly recommend any of our readers who are interested in the subject, and desire fuller details, to read Mr. Herbert's book.

Writing   We have seen, on p. 17, that Bede stated how, by the study of Scripture, the Latin tongue, and with it Roman characters, became common to the people ; but there were others. A scramasax, or knife, at the British Museum is interesting because it has the Runic characters engraved on it. This system of writing was used by the Nordic peoples, and dates back to the fourth century, but was not in general use in England after the eighth. Its angular form made it very suitable for engraving on wood or stone.

Runes are cut on the wonderful Franks casket in the Anglo-Saxon Gallery at the British Museum (Fig. 33), to explain the carvings, where Egil the archer is shown fighting his enemies ; Wayland the smith makes a drinking cup of a skull, and Romulus and Remus are with their foster-mother the Wolf. The casket is made of whalebone, and is Northumbrian work of about 700 A.D. It should be studied also for the details it gives of costume.

Another form of writing is that which employed the Ogham characters. These can be studied at the British Museum, and consisted of horizontal and diagonal strokes, and dots, grouped in series up to five, cut on the faces and edges of a tombstone for example. It is thought that the system was

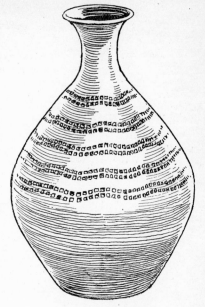

FIG. 27.—Jutish Bottle.
(British Museum.)

invented in Ireland. Bishop Forrest Browne has explained it as having arisen from the use of the five fingers, like the deaf-and-dumb language in the eighteenth century.

The British Museum contains the only known example of a tenth century Anglo-Saxon writing tablet, as Fig. 34, made of bone with sunk panels inside in which wax was spread to take the scratched writing done with a metal stylus.

Other writing was done with a reed, or quill pen, on the parchment of manuscripts or deeds. These were sealed with wax, by a bronze seal, as Fig. 35 from the British Museum, which belonged to Ethilwald, Bishop of Dunwich, whose See, or seat, has long since been swallowed up by the waves.

There is an impression of a seal, in lead, at the Museum of Coenwulf, king of Mercia, 796-819. It was a *bulla* of lead like this, attached to papal documents, which gave rise to the name of papal " bulls."

Christianity We will consider now the great part which Christianity played in civilizing the English, but first we must endeavour to put ourselves in their places. We must remember that their faith had been much the same as that of the Vikings we describe on page 67, and an eminently suitable one for the warrior. By fighting he reached Valhal, and remained there. There were no complexities, or subtleties ; the gods were like men destroyers. We must try and imagine their astonishment when Aidan, or Augustine, preached to them of the Sermon on the Mount, and told them that men were made in the image of God, and not a god like Wodan, but a God of Love ; that they could be creators. Here was a Faith which was easy to understand, and yet so difficult to live up to, because men continued, and still continue, to be more like the images of the old heathen gods they themselves had made.

We will trace all this in the pages of Bede, but first we must remember, as already stated on page 8, that the Britons were converted long before the Mission of S. Augustine, and that S. Patrick founded the Irish Church as early as **427**. There were differences between the Church of Ireland, and that of Rome, mainly as to the proper date for keeping Easter, and these were not composed until the Synod of Whitby in 664. We must not think of Rome as the only source of Christian inspiration. When Christ was born, Rome, and Roman civilization, was at a low ebb, and it was not till the Edict of Toleration, in 313, that Christianity was recognized there, but Christ was born in Palestine, and here it was in Asia Minor that the greater part of the work of the Apostles was carried out. As a result, Christianity was adopted as the State religion at Edessa, in N. Mesopotamia, as early as 202, and in Armenia at the end of the century. Bede, in the first chapter of his history, compares England with Armenia, Macedonia, Italy and other countries. This is very interesting, because Professor Strzygowski has shown, that there are striking parallels between the church architecture of Asia Minor and that evolved here in England. The church at Silchester built here in Roman times, see Part III, page 28, can be called Basilican, because it was founded on the Roman basilica, and the Saxon church of Worth, in Sussex, follows the same pattern and has an apse at the east end. If, however, we take Escomb, Durham, we find a different type of church with a square ended chancel. This latter type may have been introduced, not from Rome, but Asia Minor, and it is more usual in England than the apse.

FIG. 28.—Anglo-Saxon Cup, from Saxby, Leics. (British Museum.)

The question is were they influenced in their design by motives which travelled from Asia Minor to S. Russia in the same way as the love of colour and jewelry to which we referred on page 6. Many of the Saxon churches give the idea of timber designs carried out in stone and they brought a timber building tradition with them.

Many of the early churches must have been on the lines of the old Norwegian timber church, as Fig. 38. We deal more fully with church architecture in the next chapter.

The practice of building wayside crosses seems to have started in Saxon times. These marked the way, or the parting of the ways, or where the river could be forded, or, as a nun writing in 699 said, " it is customary among the Saxon people, on the estates of the nobles or gentry, to have for the use of those who make a point of attending daily prayers, not a church, but the sign of the Holy Cross, set up aloft and consecrated to the Lord."

Augustine came to England in 597, at the instigation of Augustine Bertha, daughter of the king of the Franks, and wife of Ethelbert, king of Kent. We shall let Bede tell the tale :

" On the east of Kent is the large Isle of Thanet, containing, according to the English way of reckoning, 600 families," which apparently was used as a sixth century Ellis Island, because here Augustine stayed until " Some days after, the king came into the island, and sitting in the open air, ordered Augustine and his companions to be brought into his presence. For he had taken precaution that they should not come to him in any house, lest, according to an ancient super- stition, if they practised any magical arts, they might impose upon him, and so get the better of him." As a result of his

41 G

preaching, Augustine was allowed to settle at Canterbury, where "there was on the east side of the city, a church dedicated to the honour ot S. Martin, built whilst the Romans were still in the island, wherein the queen, who, as has been said before, was a Christian, used to pray. In this they first began to meet, to sing, to pray, to say mass, to preach, and to baptize, till the king, being converted to the faith, allowed them to preach openly, and build or repair churches in all places."

The Roman S. Martin's appears to have consisted of a plain oblong chapel, with a semi-circular apse of which little remains now, because the western end of the present chancel was the eastern end of the original chapel, and the apse lies under the floor where the building has been extended. Bede shows that at the time of Augustine, there must have been many other Romano-British churches.

The sudden conversion of great multitudes of people, presented difficulty when they came to be baptized. Baptism was by total immersion, and as Bede tells us, "for as yet oratories, or fonts, could not be made in the early infancy of the church in these parts," so the grown-up converts flocked to the rivers and were baptized there.

Paulinus   There is a beautiful passage in Bede, dealing with the conversion of Edwin of Northumbria, in 625, by Paulinus, who was "tall of stature, a little stooping, his hair black, his visage meagre, his nose slender and aquiline, his aspect both venerable and majestic." He preached to the king, and Coifi the chief priest, urged that the old gods be deserted, "For none of your people has applied himself more diligently to the worship of our gods than I; and yet there are many who receive greater favours from you, and are more preferred than I, and are more prosperous in all their undertakings. Now if the gods were good for anything, they would rather forward me, who have been more careful to serve them." Here is a splendid illustration of the old pagan spirit of which we wrote in Part III, page 71; a bargain was made with the gods, and for the service rendered by worship, rewards were expected.

Another of the king's chief men was moved by Paulinus to a nobler strain, and said: "The present life of man, O king, seems to me, in comparison of that time which is unknown to us, like to the swift flight of a sparrow through the room wherein you sit at supper in winter, with your commanders and ministers, and a good fire in the midst, whilst the storms of rain and snow prevail abroad ; the sparrow,

Fig. 29.—Drinking Horn.
(British Museum.)

I say, flying in at one door, and immediately out at another, whilst he is within is safe from the wintry storm ; but after a short space of fair weather, he immediately vanishes out of your sight, into the dark winter from which he had emerged. So this life of man appears for a short space, but of what went before, or what is to follow, we are utterly ignorant. If, therefore, this new doctrine contains something more certain, it seems justly to deserve to be followed." This man was a poet.

Coifi, as a priest, could not carry arms and had to ride a mare, so when he threw off his allegiance to the old gods he begged for the king's stallion and arms, and girding on a sword and taking a spear, galloped to the temple and cast the spear into the temple and destroyed it ; but then Coifi was not a poet, and this was just the ungrateful thing that a realist would do.

But all the temples were not destroyed in this way. Pope Temples Gregory wrote to Abbot Mellitus, in 601, that " the temples of the idols in that nation (English) ought not to be destroyed ; but let the idols that are in them be destroyed ; let holy water be made and sprinkled in the said temples, let altars be erected and relics placed." It was this charitable outlook which saved for us to-day the Pantheon in Rome as the most complete example of the building of classical Rome. " Boniface, who came fourth after Pope Gregory, and who obtained of the Emperor Phocas that the temple called by the ancients Pantheon, as representing all the gods, should be given to the Church of Christ."

Again the Church was charitable. Pope Gregory pointed out that as the heathen English had " been used to slaughter

43

Fig. 30.—Page from the Book of Kells.   (Dublin.)

FIG. 31.—Page from Lindisfarne Gospels. (British Museum.)

FIG. 32. — Figure
from Gospels of
S. Chad.

many oxen in the sacrifices to devils, some solemnity must be exchanged for them on this account." Christianity was not to be made doleful. The festivals were to be feast days when the people could be festive. They were to be allowed " to build themselves huts of the boughs of trees, about those churches which have been turned to that use from temples, and celebrate the solemnity with religious feasting, and no more offer beasts to the Devil, but kill cattle to the praise of God in their eating."

So the good work continued until it looked as if the country were to see peace. We read that in the time of Edwin, King of Northumbria, " a woman with her new-born babe might walk throughout the island, from sea to sea, without receiving any harm. That king took such care for the good of his nation that in several places where he had seen clear springs near the highways he caused stakes to be fixed, with brass dishes hanging at them, for the convenience of travellers." But the fight was not won yet. Edwin was killed at the battle of Hatfield, by invading Mercians under Penda, who was still pagan. Paulinus fled to the south, and his work was largely undone.

Now we come to the very special service which the Church of Ireland rendered to the Christian cause. Oswald, the king who succeeded to the throne of Northumbria, had passed some part of his youth in the monastery of Iona, which, as we have seen on page 8, was founded by Columba, who went there from Ireland about 563, and it was to Iona that Oswald sent for help. They sent him, in 635, " Bishop Aidan, a man of singular meekness, piety, and moderation ; zealous in the cause of God, though not altogether according to knowledge ; for he was wont to keep Easter Sunday according to the custom of his country." This was the old quarrel.

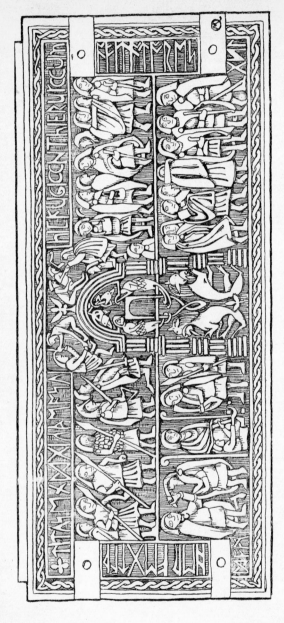

FIG. 33.—Back of Franks Casket. Carved in whale's bone. Northumbrian work, about 700 A.D.
(British Museum.)

Aidan

FIG. 34.—Bone Writing-tablet
from Blythburgh, Suffolk.
(British Museum.)

Oswald appointed Aidan to his episcopal see in the Isle of Lindisfarne, which we call Holy Island for this reason, and he was successful in his work of reconversion. We read in Bede that many religious men and women, stirred by the example of Aidan, "adopted the custom of fasting on Wednesdays and Fridays, till the ninth hour, throughout the year, except during the fifty days after Easter." Later on, in 664, the differences between the two churches were composed, and Theodore "was the first archbishop whom all the English Church obeyed."

The conversion of the South Saxons occurred at an even later date. Bede tells how Bishop Wilfrid went to Sussex, in 681, and found the inhabitants in great distress. He baptized 250 men and women slaves, and "not only rescued them from the servitude of the Devil, but gave them their bodily liberty also, and exempted them from the yoke of human servitude."

He put heart into them. A dreadful famine ensued on three years drought, so that often "forty or fifty men, being spent with want, would go together to some precipice, or to the seashore, and there, hand in hand, perish by the fall, or be swallowed up by the waves." This was while they were heathen, because on the very day the nation was baptized rain fell. The bishop not only saved their souls, but "taught them to get their food by fishing; for their sea and rivers abounded in fish, but the people had no skill to take them, except eels alone. The bishop's men having gathered eel-nets everywhere, cast them into the sea, and by the blessing of God took three hundred fishes of several sorts." Wilfrid founded a monastery at Selsey, the Island of the Sea-Calf. Earlier there had been a small monastery of Irish monks at Bosham, " but none of the natives cared either to follow their course of life, or hear their preaching."

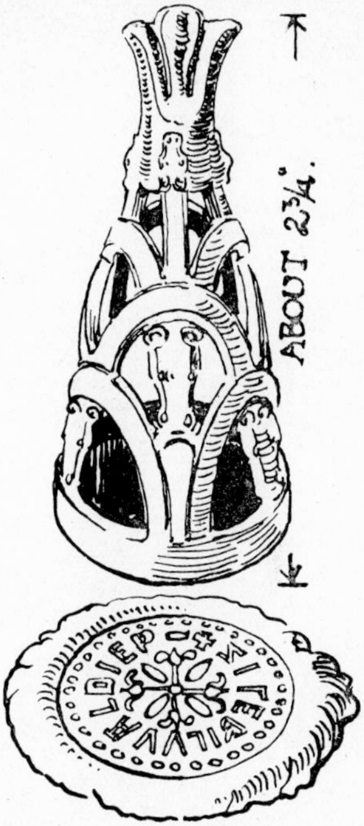

The early Church was tremendously concerned in keeping its members to the true Faith, and it had to combat the heretics who would have divided it up into many small sects. Had this happened, the assault on heathendom would have failed, and with the failure, the history of Western Europe would have been different. The Greek Church, which is a federation of many eastern churches, of which the most important is the Church of Russia, remained in communion with the Church of Rome until 1054.

Again the Church was compelled to interest itself in temporal affairs. The Popes

Wilfrid

FIG. 35.—Bronze Seal of Ethilwald, Bishop of Dunwich, about 850, from Eye, Suffolk. (British Museum.)

wrote to the Kings, and urged them to lead Christian lives, and the Pope signed himself, " the servant of the servants of God." Pope Boniface, in 625, wrote to King Edwin, and sent him " a shirt, with one gold ornament, and one garment of Ancyra," and to Queen Ethelberga "a silver looking-glass, and gilt ivory comb."

The bishops were rewarded. Pope Gregory sent the Pall to Augustine. The Pall, or pallium, was a long strip of fine woollen cloth, ornamented with crosses, the middle of which was formed with a loose collar resting on the shoulders, while the extremities before and behind hung down nearly to the feet.

H

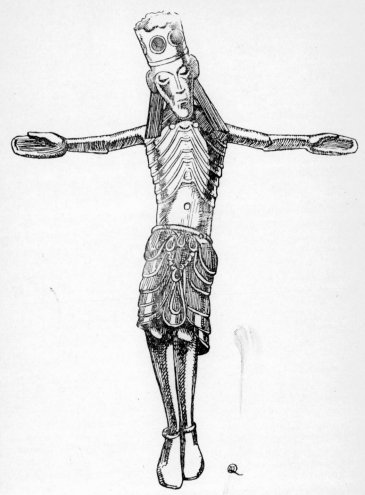

FIG. 36.—Figure of Christ, in bronze. (Irish. British Museum.)

It would be well for us perhaps to try and catch a little of the spirit which animated these men in their fight, because it was as a fight against the powers of darkness that they regarded their work. If they held a Bible in one hand, in the other there was a sword.

Augustine summoned a conference, in 603, to which the bishops of the Britons were invited, and at which the date of Easter was discussed. Augustine wrought a miracle restoring a blind man's sight, after the British bishops had failed, to convince them that his church was in the right ; but they remained unconvinced. Bede then tells how " the man of God, Augustine, is said, in a threatening manner, to have foretold, that in case they would not join in unity with their brethren, they should be warred upon by their enemies ; and, if they would not preach the way of life to the English nation, they should at their hands undergo the vengeance of death." This is what happened. The Britons were defeated by the English, at Chester, with great slaughter, and 1,200 monks from Bangor were among the slain. There was not much love lost between them. Even Bede refers to the Britons as " that perfidious nation."

Bede gives a beautiful vision of what the seventh century man was given to expect after death. A Northumbrian rose from the dead, and related the things which he had seen. " He that led me had a shining countenance and a bright garment, and we went on silently, as I thought,

British Christians

Fig. 37. — Figure in Bronze. (Irish. British Museum.)

Fig. 38.—Old Timber-framed Church at Urnes, Sogn, Norway.
XIth Century.

towards the north-east.   Walking on, we came to a vale of
great breadth and depth, but of infinite length ; on the
left it appeared full of dreadful flames, the other side was
no less horrid for violent hail and cold snow flying in all
directions ; both places were full of men's souls, which
seemed by turns to be tossed from one side to the other, as
it were by a violent storm ; for when the wretches could no
longer endure the excess of heat, they leaped into the middle
of the cutting cold ; and finding no rest there, they leaped
back again into the middle of the unquenchable flames "—
the guide said, " this is not the hell you imagine."

They passed on to a place where—" As we went on through
the shades of night, on a sudden there appeared before us

frequent globes of black flames, rising as it were out of a great pit, and falling back again into the same. When I had been conducted thither, my leader suddenly vanished, and left me alone in the midst of darkness and this horrid vision, whilst those same globes of fire, without intermission, at one time flew up and at another fell back into the bottom of the abyss ; and I observed that all the flames, as they ascended, were full of human souls, which, like sparks flying up with smoke, were sometimes thrown on high, and again, when the vapour of the fire ceased, dropped down into the depth below."

Turning towards the south-east, and coming to the top of a vast wall, they found within it a delightful field, full of fragrant flowers. " In this field were innumerable assemblies of men in white, and many companies seated together rejoicing." The Northumbrian was told : " This is not the kingdom of heaven, as you imagine."

When he had passed farther on he " discovered before me a much more beautiful light, and therein heard sweet voices of people singing, and so wonderful a fragrancy proceeded from the place, that the other which I had before thought most delicious, then seemed to me very indifferent ; even as that extraordinary brightness of the flowery field, compared with this, appeared mean and inconsiderable." But beyond this they were not allowed to pass.

The guide then told the Northumbrian what were the places he had seen. The dreadful vale was the place " in which the souls of those are tried and

Fig. 39.—Ornament, Urnes Church.

punished, who, delaying to confess their crimes, at length have recourse to repentance at the point of death," but after punishment they were received into the Kingdom of Heaven.

The fiery pit was the mouth of Hell, " into which whosoever falls shall never be delivered to all eternity."

The first flowery field was the place for those who were " not so perfect as to deserve to be immediately admitted into the Kingdom of Heaven ; yet they shall all, at the day of judgment, see Christ, and partake of the joys of His kingdom ; for whoever are perfect in thought, word and deed, as soon as they depart the body, immediately enter into the Kingdom of Heaven ; in the neighbourhood whereof that place is, where you heard the sound of sweet singing, with the fragrant odour and bright light."

If this were a passionate belief with men, it is an explanation why, in religious persecution, it was held not to be a bad thing even to destroy a man's body, if in so doing you saved his soul.

FIG. 40.—The Ruthwell Cross. Partial reconstruction. Cross is now inside Ruthwell Church, Dumfriesshire.

CHAPTER II

THE COMING OF THE VIKINGS

S O far as this part is concerned, we shall deal with the history of our country, between 815, when the Britons were finally conquered by the Saxons under Ecgberht, K. of Wessex, up to the final conquest of the Saxons by the Danes under Canute in 1016, and then on to the Norman Invasion in 1066.

We shall be concerned with the doings of the Danes, Norsemen, or Northmen, who raided our land as Vikings. To go viking meant to go adventuring. We can read in the Burnt Njal Saga, how Gunnar went a sea-roving. He had become tired of a stay-at-home life, so sailed away with Hallvard the White to discover new things. In reading of their ventures we must put off the horn-rims of the twentieth century, or we shall condemn them as pirates and be quite wrong. Obviously it was a perfectly respectable proceeding to go viking. It meant fighting, of course, but fighting was a principal occupation. It meant annexing the goods of the conquered, but that was part of the game. With gentlemen named Eric Bloodaxe, Harold Wartooth, Wolf the Unwashed, and Thorkel the Skull-splitter, a certain roughness must be expected ; but let there be no mistake, they were the gentlemen of the day.

The story of Burnt Njal is published in Everyman's Library, and should be read because it is full of life and colour.

It was not till 787 that the Vikings turned their attention to this country. We read in the Anglo-Saxon Chronicle, that in this year, " first came three ships of Northmen, out of Haerethaland (Denmark). And then the reve (sheriff) rode out to the place, and would have driven them to the King's town, because he knew not who they were : and

FIG. 41.—Font in Deerhurst Church, Gloucestershire. When set up again in the church the ornament of base was placed immediately under the bowl.

I

they there slew him. These were the first ships of Danish-men who sought the land of the English nation."

" God's church at Lindisfarne " was destroyed in 793, and Jarrow 794. There appear to have been two lines of attack. The first was from the Danes and Gotas who lived around the Wick, or Vik, now the fjord of Christiania. A glance at the map will show how easily they could come S. by hugging the shore, and then crossing to the Thames, work down the Channel. The second line was from Norway to Shetland, and then S. on either side of Scotland, to Northumbria on one hand, and Ireland on the other.

The Vikings occupied Ireland for about two centuries, and were differentiated there, because the Norsemen were known as the white strangers (*Finn-Gaill*), and the Danes as the dark strangers (*Dubh-Gaill*).

We know all these things ; they are the commonplaces of history. What we do not really understand, is how it came about that this Northern people should in the first place have felt the tremendous necessity for movement, and then have been so well equipped that they were able to carry out their schemes. There must have been some great idea and commander ; some spiritual urge at work.

Norway was called Haloga-land, and the country bred the people who lived there. It is like a long, rocky, ice-clad saw, with the sea running up between the teeth. Around the fjords are only small patches of fertile soil ; so men were forced to the sea to fish, and trade, and fight ; but where did they learn the art of combination ? In Burnt Njal they are a quarrelsome people, continually fighting amongst themselves, but yet cool-headed enough to leave off and go to Law if need be.

Three ships came in 787, but in 833 as many as 35 came to Charmouth, and by 851, 350 came to the mouth of the Thames. We cannot follow all their movements here, but Wales, Ireland, and France were all raided. One important detail is that Rurik, King of Sweden, founded the kingdom of Russia at the end of the ninth century. In this way the Vikings reached Kief, and from here went to take service with the Emperor at Constantinople, and fought in Asia Minor against the Saracens.

Harald Sigurdsson, son of Sigurd Syr, King of Norway,

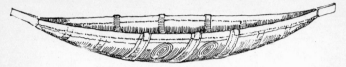

FIG. 42.—Prehistoric Ship Models.

did this, and later became King of Norway as Harald Haardraade. Always something seems to happen when the Northern peoples rub shoulders with the old civilisations of the Near East. The Vikings brought back with them the rarest of commodities, ideas, and we have to admit that they were an extraordinary people.

Roman power was based on the legionary, but the Viking was the first to realize the meaning of Sea-Power. No other nation had a navy comparable to theirs. So we can take it that their land drove them to the sea, and then the sea civilised them. It made them learn to pull together, because life on board ship is impossible unless you do, and they carried the lesson ashore with them, and fought together. Their ships were beautifully designed and very speedy, so when they sailed up the rivers, so conveniently arranged for them on our East Coast, they took horses, put their webbed feet in stirrups, and rode through the country. They were like evil will-o'-the wisps, never where the Saxons expected to find them. The English ceorl, called up by the fyrd of the shire, was thinking of his crops, and armed only with spear and shield, was opposed to the Viking with steel cap and ring-mail shirt, who, as a mounted infantry man, could deliver his blow when, and where, he liked.

This will be a good place in which to write of the Viking ship. If we turn back the pages of history, as we did in Part III, pp. 2-16, we find how often some new idea has revolutionised the lives and liberties of the peoples. Armour, the bow, horse, military engineering, and the walled city, were all used in warfare long before the days of Christ. It is part of the horrid tale of men eagerly seeking for new weapons with which to conquer and oppress their neighbours. The Vikings had the wonderful ship which the stormy waters and the seafaring genius of their people had deve-

The Viking Ship

FIG. 43.—On Board the Gokstad Ship.

loped. The Norseman had evidently used the sea from a very early date. Fig. 42 shows a small boat 4 inches to 5 inches long discovered in an urn at Nors, N. Jutland, in 1885. There were about 100 of these packed one into another, they were made of bronze, plated inside and out with thin sheet gold, and must date from the Bronze Age. Obviously they are the forerunners of the later Viking ships. We know what these were like, because the old Vikings loved their boats so well that they were buried in them. We saw on page 20 how in Beowulf the dead Scyld was placed in his ship, and pushed off to sail away into the unknown. In another type of funeral the body was placed in the ship and both burned together. A third type is more useful to the archaeologists, because here the ship was pulled up on to land, and the dead body placed in it, with all the articles which the warrior would need in the spirit world. Then over the whole a barrow of earth was piled to remain for excavation in our time.

Our illustrations Figs. 43 and 44 have been drawn from the boat discovered at Gokstad, near Sandefjord, on the Fjord of Christiania. It was a beautiful idea and shows

how the Viking loved his ship : in the Sagas he calls it the
" Reindeer of the breezes," the " Horse of gull's track,"
the " Raven of the wind," and many other equally poetic
names.

Shall we conjure up the burial scene ? The ship drawn
up, its prow pointing to the sea ; a salt breeze blowing in,
stinging the nostrils and singing in the rigging. The pro-
cession from the Hall, the dead Viking borne by his warriors,
the body stiff and cold but dressed and armed for his last
voyage. Then the slaughter of the terrified horses and
whimpering dogs who were to accompany their master.
Overhead, attracted by the smell of blood, the wheeling,
screaming gulls, like valkyries sent by Odin as an escort
to Valhal. Some such scene was staged around the Gokstad
ship in the beginning.

The ship was clinker built, with overlapping planks of
oak. About 78 feet long, her beam was 16 feet 7 inches,
and depth 6 feet 9 inches. She had more beam than is
generally imagined (see Fig. 44). The one square sail was
useful before the wind, and at other times there were
sixteen oars for pulling on each side. The mast was stepped
as shown in Fig. 43, and kept in position by a heavy slab
dropped into a slot ; it was lowered aft by slacking off
the forestay. The steering was by a shaped rudder, or
steerboard, hence the term starboard. The lines of hull
were as beautiful as those of a modern yacht, and just as
scientifically modelled, so as to offer the minimum resistance
to the passage through the water. At night a tilt was put
up as Fig. 44. Fig. 45 is of one of the wooden beds found
on the Gokstad ship. Made of oak, it is ingeniously constructed so that it could be taken to pieces. The posts are
2 feet 3 inches high ; the ends 3 feet 5 inches wide, and the
sides 7 feet 5 inches long. Only the chiefs would have had beds.

There is a note in William of Malmesbury bearing on
boats. Godwin gave Hardicanute " a ship beaked with gold,
having eighty soldiers on board, who had two bracelets on
either arm, each weighing sixteen ounces of gold ; on their
heads were gilt helmets ; on their left shoulder they carried
a Danish axe, with an iron spear in their right hand."

The Anglo-Saxon Chronicle (891) gives details of other
boats in use at the time of far more primitive build—" And

SECTION AMIDSHIPS.

FIG. 44.—The Gokstad Ship with Tilt up at Night.

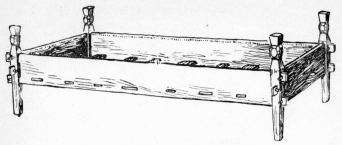

Fig. 45.—Bed from the Gokstad Ship.

three Scots (Irish) came to King Alfred in a boat without any oars from Ireland, whence they had stolen away. . . . The boat in which they came was made of two hides and a half." This sounds like a sea-curragh made of wicker and covered with hide as the coracle. An interesting seventeenth century print of such a boat is given in an article by Mr. Nance in the *Mariner's Mirror*, vol. viii, 117.

We can now return to the doings of the Vikings on land. Asser tells a tale which shows that the Saxons credited them with supernatural powers. " They say, moreover, that in every battle, wherever that flag went before them, if they were to gain the victory a live crow would appear flying in the middle of the flag ; but if they were doomed to be defeated it would hang down motionless, and this was often proved so."

When they came to settle in the land, after the Peace of Wedmore, in 878, they showed great judgment in the selection of their five strongholds or burgs. The English had avoided the Roman roads, but the Vikings knew the importance of transport and they selected points which could easily be reached by land or water. Lincoln was on the River Witham, at the junction of the Roman Fosse Way, and Ermine Street. Stamford on Ermine Street, and the River Welland. Leicester on the Fosse Way, and the River Soar. Derby on the River Derwent, and Ryknield Street, and Nottingham on the Trent.

When the Vikings were established in the Danelaw, they doubtless sent for their wives, and children, and living together in the fortified burgs, re-established the custom of city life.

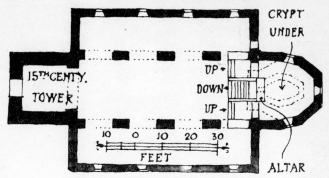

Fig. 46.—Plan, Wing Church, Bucks.

We use By-law to-day, because it comes from the Scandinavian *by-lor*, or city law. Towns having the same termination as Whitby, were probably founded by the Danes. In Mr. Collingwood's interesting book on Scandinavian Britain, many survivals of Norse are given in the dialects of Cumberland and Westmoreland. To berry (*berja*, thresh); the boose (*báss*, cow-shed); galt (*galti*, a pig); garn (*garn*, yarn); handsel (*handsöl*, bargain), and many others.

Where the Vikings settled, the land was divided into trithings, wapentakes and carucates. In Domesday these measurements are applied to Nottingham, Leicester, Derby, Rutland, and Lincoln. Twelve carucates equal one hundred. The duodecimal, 12, seems to have come from the Dane, and the long hundred of 120 is a survival from their times. Another interesting detail is found in Domesday, where more freemen are mentioned in the Danelaw, than elsewhere, and the men of that part, still perhaps think of themselves as being sturdier in thought and action than their Saxon cousins of the South.

The names of the Things, or Assemblies, of which we read in Burnt Njal, survive in names like the Suffolk hundred of Thingoe, or Tinghowe, Tingewick, near Buckingham, and Tingrith, South Beds.

But if the arrival of the Vikings was an advantage in one way, in that it stiffened the fibre of the race, in another it was fraught with great peril. When they first came, in 787, they were pagans, and the delicate fabric of Christianity was

Fig. 47.—Interior, Wing Church, Bucks. (Partial reconstruction.)

FIG. 48.—East End, Wing Church, Bucks. (Partial reconstruction.)

torn down and trampled in the dust. Churches were destroyed, monasteries plundered, and the civilization of the country put back centuries.

Viking Gods   Odin, Thor and Frey were the greatest of their gods. Odin, the God of Wisdom, was the chief, and the same as the Anglo-Saxon Wodan. Tall and bearded, he loved war, and his two

66

ravens, Hugin and Munin, brought him news of men. He had one eye, having sacrificed the other to drink wisdom at the Well of Mimir. As the Chief of the gods he had a hall, Valhal. The Valkyries were his attendants, and the choosers of the dead. Virgin goddesses, armed with helmet, shield and spear, and mounted on horseback, they rode through the air, over the rainbow, the celestial bridge which gods and men must tread

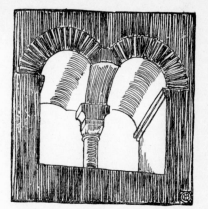

Fig. 49.—Window, Wing Church.

to reach Valhal. Only those who died in battle, were chosen, and taken back to feast with Odin, to find their pastime in fighting and their reward in that they always lived on to feast, and fight, another day. The sorry souls who died in their beds, never reached Valhal, but went instead to *Hel*. Ty was the God of War, and Thor, the Thunder God, protected farmers and threw his hammer, which is the thunderbolt. The gods accepted the sacrifice of horses, oxen, sheep and boars, but in times of great trouble their will was found by casting lots, and men were killed to appease them. This was the animating faith of the Vikings, who nearly conquered the world of their day, and whose blood still flows in English veins.

The period of this second part of our book was a tragic one Alfred for the Saxons in England, the gloom of which was only dispelled by the gallant stand made by Alfred. He turned his levy into a militia, part of which was always on duty ; he fortified burgs and improved his fleet. He not only protected England in his time, but laid the foundations of a power which was to conquer her yet again in 1066. Some of the Northmen, Norsemen, or Normans, finding that Alfred's fleet really did mean business, turned their attention to Gaul, where they eventually settled down, in 912, founding Normandy.

FIG. 50.—Worth, Sussex.

The Franks did not find them particularly pleasant neighbours. William of Malmesbury tells how Charles, King of the Franks, finding that he could not beat the Normans,

68

proposed to them that they should hold the land they had already conquered as his vassals. Rollo thought it over, and " the inbred and untamable ferocity of the man may well be imagined, for, on receiving this gift, as the bystanders suggested to him that he ought to kiss the foot of his benefactor, disdaining to kneel down, he seized the king's foot and dragged it to his mouth as he stood erect. The king falling on his back, the Normans began to laugh, and the Franks to be indignant."

Fig. 51.—Worth, Sussex : Nave Windows.

This is an interesting passage. History was repeating itself. Long years before, the Franks and Saxons had descended on the Gauls and Britons and treated them in much the same way ; now they themselves were helpless before the Vikings. Just as the Gauls and Britons had learned to lean on the strong arm of Rome, and could not stand alone when it was withdrawn, so the Franks and Saxons found civilized life enervating. They began to put on airs. Ethelwulf, the father of Alfred, traced his descent by way of Cerdic to Woden and " Bedwig of Sceaf, that is, the son of Noah, he was born in Noah's Ark." Other Bible characters were worked in to " Adam the first man, and our Father, that is, Christ "—and the Vikings came and laughed.

We do not concern ourselves very much with the doings of kings, because generally they are so remote from everyday life, but this cannot be said of Alfred ; perhaps that is why his name lives. Here was a king who, though kingly, had touched adversity and known trouble.

There are two tales which are well known, but explain

Fig. 52.—Exterior of Church, Bradford-on-Avon, Wilts.

Fig. 53.—Interior of Bradford-on-Avon Church, Wilts.

FIG. 54.—Sculpture, Bradford-on-Avon, Wilts.

why he had such a hold on his people. Asser tells one, of how when the king had taken refuge in a hut " it happened on a certain day, that the countrywoman, wife of the cow-herd, was preparing some loaves to bake, and the king, sitting at the hearth, made ready his bow and other warlike instruments. The unlucky woman espying the cakes burning at the fire, ran up to remove them," and gave the king a little bit of her mind, telling him that if he wanted to eat the cakes, he might at least have watched them.

The other tale is told by William of Malmesbury, of the time when Alfred was hard pressed at Athelney : " Not long after, venturing from his concealment, he hazarded an experiment of consummate art. Accompanied only by one of his most faithful adherents, he entered the tent of the Danish king under the disguise of a minstrel ; and being admitted, as a professor of the mimic art, to the banqueting room, there was no object of secrecy that he did not minutely attend to, both with eyes and ears."

But even Alfred's genius could only maintain a hold on the S.W. of England, and by the Peace of Wedmore, 878, Northumbria, half of Mercia, and E. Anglia became the Danelaw. We must find out more about Alfred because, if we obtain a picture of the Saxons at their best from Bede, under Alfred and his immediate descendants they made a good fight before they were swamped by the Danes.

Asser the historian, who lived at the court of Alfred, tells us that he " remained illiterate even till he was twelve years old or more ; but he listened with serious attention to the

Fɪɢ. 55.—Tower of Earls Barton Church, Northants.   (Partial reconstruction.)

L

Saxon poems which he often heard recited." His father Ethelwulf sent him to Rome, in 853, and took him there again in 855. Notwithstanding the advantages of foreign travel, as late as 884 " he had not yet learned to read anything."

When Alfred became king, he paid great attention to education. He imported Johannes Scotus from France to assist, but the school boys do not seem to have taken to him kindly, because we are told that he " was pierced with the iron styles of the boys he was instructing."

Alfred did not suffer from his own lack of schooling, because we read that he " was affable and pleasant to all, and curiously eager to investigate things unknown." This being the case, the king determined to acquire knowledge, and then pass it on to his subjects. He realized that History, to be of any real use to a people, must have an international flavour about it, and not be too self-consciously national ; nations are like individuals and must rub shoulders.

Alfred therefore took " The History of the World, from the Creation to 416," by Orosius, a Spaniard, and caused it to be translated into Anglo-Saxon, and while this was being done he inserted accounts by Ohthere, and Wulfstan. This was one of the first of the Outlines.

Travels Ohthere was a Norseman, who, following the adventurous habit of his people, had come to England, and taken service in the Saxon Court. " Ohthere told his lord, King Alfred, that he dwelt northmost of all Northmen." He was one of the first explorers. " He said, that, at a certain time, he wished to find out how far the land lay right north ; or whether any man dwelt to the north of the waste. Then he went right north near the land : he left, all the way, the waste land on the right, and the wide sea on the left, for three days. Then was he as far north as whale-hunters ever go. He then went yet right north, as far as he could sail in the next three days. Then the land bent there right east, or the sea in on the land, he knew not whether ; but he knew hat he there waited for a western wind, or a little to the n .th, and sailed thence east near the land, as far as he could sail in four days. Then he must wait there for a right north wind, because the land bent there right south, or the sea in on the land, he knew not whether. Then sailed he thence right south, near the land, as far as he could sail in five days."

74

Ohthere had rounded the North Cape, and reached the White Sea. He found the Biarmians living on the shore there, and hunted horse-whales (walruses), "because they have very good bone in their teeth . . . and their hides are very good for ship-ropes."

Ohthere was a wealthy man in his own country, having 600 reindeer, 20 horned cattle, 20 sheep, and 20 swine.

We must imagine Alfred and his men sitting around the fire at night, listening to this tale of adventure. It may have been Ohthere who gave him the idea, that the only way to check the Vikings, was to beat them at their own game. We read in the Anglo-Saxon Chronicle : " Then King Alfred commanded long-ships to be built to oppose the esks ; they were full nigh twice as long as the others ; some had sixty oars, and some had more ; they were both swifter and steadier, and also higher than the others. They were shapen neither like the Frisian nor the Danish, but so as it seemed to him they would be most efficient." *Alfred's ships*

Alfred was a great builder in other ways. He repaired London in 886. This raises a very interesting problem. Did he repair, and rebuild London, in the Roman manner ? Even to-day, if we go to Bath, we find very impressive remains of classical architecture. There is the pediment of the Temple of Sul, and the Great Bath itself. In Alfred's time there must have been many buildings which were nearly perfect, and he may have restored these. This is suggested by Asser, who wrote, " What shall I say of the cities and towns which he restored . . . of the royal vills constructed of stone, removed from their old site, and handsomely rebuilt." This would explain why in some of the old manuscripts, buildings are shown which look as if they had been transplanted from Italy. The Saxons would not have been able to originate a classical building, but they may have restored them. In any picture then of Saxon London, side by side with their timber Halls, we must be prepared for these old Roman buildings given a new lease of life by Alfred's genius.

Asser tells how he encouraged people " to build houses, majestic and good, beyond all the precedents of his ancestors, by his new mechanical inventions." Whether these were wood or stone we do not know, but he built a church at Athelney on what was regarded as a new plan. He planted *Building*

Earls barton ch. Northants. Tower Doorway. June ''

FIG. 56.—Tower Doorway, Earls
Barton Church, Northants.

four posts in the ground, which formed the angles of the main structure, and around these built four aisles. This must have resembled the old Norwegian timber framed church shown in Fig. 38, and was not at all classical, but entirely northern in conception.

A note in the Anglo-Saxon Chronicle of a little later (978) suggests that the Hall had been moved up to what we should now call the first floor level, where it was to remain until the fourteenth century —" In this year all the chief ' Witan ' of the English nation fell at Calne from an upper chamber, except the holy archbishop Dunstan, who alone supported himself upon a beam."

Neither houses nor churches were very comfortable. Asser tells how the king caused six candles to be made, out of 72 pennyweights of wax ; each candle had twelve divisions, and lasted four hours, so that the six candles lasted through the 24 hours. But, owing to the " violence of the wind, which blew day and night without intermission through the doors and windows of the churches," the candles guttered and did not keep correct time, so the king " ordered a lantern to be beautifully constructed of wood and white ox-horn." The water-clocks of which we wrote on page 109, Part II, and page 67, Part III, must have been forgotten.

With the candles, Alfred " so divided the twenty-four hours of the day and night as to employ eight of them in writing,

76

in reading, and in prayer, eight in the refreshment of his body, and eight in dispatching the business of his realm."

He had need to safeguard his time in this way, because there was so much for him to do. Laws had to be made. William of Malmesbury tells us how Alfred "appointed centuries, which they call 'hundreds,' and decennaries, that is to say, 'tythings,' so that every Englishman living, according to law, must be a member of both. If anyone was accused of a crime, he was obliged immediately to produce persons from the hundred and tything to become his surety ; and whosoever was unable to find such surety, must dread the severity of the laws. If any who was impleaded made his escape either before or after he had found surety, all persons of the hundred and tything paid a fine to the king. By this regulation he diffused such peace through the country, that he ordered golden bracelets, which might mock the eager desires of the passengers while no one durst take them away, to be hung up on the public causeways, where the roads crossed each other."

The personal combat was another method of settling differences. In 1041, we read of William Malmesbury, that Gunhilda, sister of Hardecanute, and wife of Henry, Emperor of the Germans, was accused of adultery—"She opposed in single contest to her accuser, a man of gigantic size, a young lad of her brother's establishment, whom she had brought from England, while her other attendants held back in cowardly apprehension. When, therefore, they engaged, the impeacher, through the miraculous interposition of God, was worsted, by being ham-strung."

Alfred appears to have been content to concentrate the power of Wessex within its own borders, and it was left to his successors to carry war into the Danelaw. They were so successful, that under Eadred, and then Eadgar, with the assistance of Dunstan, the Danelaw submitted, and England became one kingdom ; then came decline, and by the days of Aethelred the Unready, 978-1016, the whole of England passed into Danish hands. The dismal tale can be traced in the Chronicle. "In that year (991) it was decreed that tribute, for the first time, should be given to the Danish men, on account of the great terror which they caused by the sea coast ; that was at first ten thousand pounds." In 994 it was 16,000, and in 1002, 24,000 pounds of money.

Saxon Decline

In 1005 " was the great famine thoughout the English nation ; such, that no man ever before recollected one so grim." 1009 was a tragic year. A navy had been built by a levy, " from three hundred hides and from ten hides, one vessel ; and from eight hides, a helmet and a coat of mail." The ships were brought together at Sandwich but the whole business was wrecked by treachery and incapacity and " they let the whole nation's toil thus lightly pass away " so that when the Danes came again they ravaged and plundered as before, the people of East Kent paying 3,000 pounds. " Then the king commanded the whole nation to be called out ; so that they should be opposed on every side : but lo ! nevertheless, they marched as they pleased."

The Chronicle contains a terrible picture of the death of Saxon Archbishop Elphege at the hands of the Danes. "And there they then shamefully slaughtered him : they cast upon him bones and the horns of oxen, and then one of them struck him with an axe-iron on the head, so that with the blow he sank down." But enough of Destruction. We will turn to the more pleasant task of writing of Construction, and fortunately for us, in the days between Alfred, and Dunstan, there is an ample store of material on which to draw.

Church Building — This will be a convenient place in which to talk of Church building.

Fig. 46 is the plan, and Fig. 47 the Interior of Wing Church, Bucks. If reference is made to Figs. 23, 24 and 25, Part III, it will be seen that the Christian Church, which was built at Silchester, was called basilican, because it resembled the Basilica, or Hall of Justice, there. This Roman tradition of building was adopted at Wing, but the apse is polygonal, instead of being semi-circular as at Silchester. We think it is later than the Nave, and Fig. 48 shows how the exterior has the narrow strips of stone, which are characteristic of some Saxon buildings. The apse covers the crypt, or confessio, where saintly men were buried, and this was so arranged that it could be seen into from the Nave, and from openings on the outside. These crypts developed from the practice of worshipping in the Catacombs at Rome at the graves of the early martyrs.

It also led to the bad practice of burying ordinary people

S. Benet's Ch. Cambridge. Tower Arch.

C.W.69

FIG. 57.

within the church. Prof. Baldwin Brown quotes an amusing West Country epitaph bearing on this :

> " Here lie I by the chancel door,
> Here lie I because I'm poor ;
> The further in the more you pay,
> Here lie I, as warm as they."

Fig. 49 shows a window opening at Wing, with the curious mid-wall shaft, which was the forerunner of the traceried window. The next step is shown in Fig. 70.

Fig. 50 of Worth Church, Sussex, shows another Saxon Church of basilican type, with an apsidal E. end. In the typical basilica, the bishop's chair stood in the centre of the apse, and the clergy sat on a bench around the wall. The altar stood on the chord of the apse. The Choir was in front of the altar, with the catechumens, or those who were being instructed in the Nave. The women sat in one aisle, the men in the other, and the penitents were in the porch.

Figs. 52, 53 and 54, of the Saxon Church at Bradford-on-Avon, Wilts, show the type of plan with a square ended chancel, which was to become the more usual English type of church. The basilica came from Rome, and this type would seem to have its origin in the North, where most of the work of the Irish missionaries was done.

When the Saxons first began to build in stone, they imitated many of the details of timber buildings. This is very apparent in the Tower at Earls Barton, Northants, shown in Fig. 55. Great care was taken here to cut back the masonry, so that only the narrow strips of stone were visible, and the walls between were plastered. The angle quoins built with alternate long and short stones, are another typical Saxon detail. The Towers of Saxon Churches appear to have been used to house the sacristans on the first floor, to which access was gained by a wooden ladder. There were openings in the east wall of the Tower which enabled the sacristan to keep watch over the church.

In the basilican churches the porch, or narthex, at first extended right across the width of the church, as Fig. 23, Part III. Later it was abbreviated into a western porch, and this was then raised into a Tower. Fig. 56 shows the Tower doorway at Earls Barton, and how one of the stone strips was curved around it. Fig. 57 of the Tower arch at S. Benet's Church, Cambridge, from the Nave, shows this same detail on a larger

Sompling. Sussex
Tower arch
June '25. CHR.

Fig. 58.—Tower Arch, Sompting Church, Sussex.

scale, as well as the opening over from which the sacristan could look down into the church from his room in the Tower.

Fig. 58 shows the very fine Tower arch at Sompting, Sussex, and Fig. 59 of the exterior is interesting as it is the only Saxon tower in England which has its original form of roof.

The ordinary churches were timber built. Edwin was baptized at York in 627 "in the Church of S. Peter the Apostle, which he himself had built of timber . . . but as soon as he was baptized, he took care, by the direction of the same Paulinus, to build in the same place a larger and nobler church of stone, in the midst whereof that same oratory which he had first erected should be enclosed." So the wooden oratory was the forerunner of the present cathedral.

Bells   Bells were used in churches. Bede tells how a nun on the night of S. Hilda's death, " on a sudden heard the well-known sound of a bell in the air, which used to awake and call them to prayers."

The British Museum possesses an interesting relic in the iron bell of S. Cuilleann, which was enshrined in bronze in the eleventh century. Evidently the early saints used ordinary cow-bells to summon their people, and these later became sacred relics. Their walking sticks were treasured and cased in metal became the type for the pastoral staff of a bishop.

Lack of space prevents us from dealing more fully with church architecture, but readers who are interested should consult the books of Prof. Baldwin Brown we mention in our list of Authorities. The sketches we have given are sufficient to show that the art of the Saxon builder was sturdy and vigorous, and as the greater part of it is found in the E. and Midland counties, some of the credit must be given to the Danes and Vikings who settled in these parts. It should be remembered that we have to judge the builders by their smaller churches ; the larger cathedrals were pulled down, and rebuilt by the Normans.

Christian Symbols   Christianity meant the introduction of a new set of symbols into the world ; these were very necessary when many people could not read. Heraldry was a form of symbolism, and also the later tradesmen's signs. The Church used the fish as a symbol of the Saviour, because the initials of the Greek words for " Jesus Christ, Son of God, Saviour," form the Greek word for fish. The Church was shown as a ship in which the faithful sailed safely across the sea of life, and Hope was typified as an anchor. Christ was the Good Shepherd, and the Devil a serpent. The soul of the departed was shown as a dove, and Victory as a palm branch ; Immortality by a peacock ; the Resurrection by the phoenix, and the soul thirsting for baptism as a stag. The triangle was the Trinity. The sacred monogram, or *Chi-Rho* was formed of the first two letters of the Greek word for Christ. The Cross itself was used as a symbol in varying forms. The Tau, as Fig. 80, from the Greek character T. The S. Andrews like the Latin numeral X. The Latin Cross with the longer lower limb. The Evangelists were shown as Angel, Lion, Ox, and Eagle.

Then there is the Swastika, 卐, that enigmatical character which has been used from pre-historic times up till to-day.

Monasticism was introduced into this country in Saxon times. The practice was first begun by the anchorites, who in Egypt, in the third century, withdrew to the desert to pass their life in solitude and devotion. S. Pachomius organized them into a community at Tabennisi, near Denderah, 315-20, and this led to the Coptic and Abyssinian churches. The next development was in Syria, early in the fourth century, and, in the latter half, S. Basil, of Caesarea, instituted a system in Cappadocia. About 500, S. Benedict founded the great system, which bears his name, at the monastery of Monte Cassino, between Rome and Naples, which was to exercise so enormous an influence. Here in England, in Saxon times, the Rule was not followed with great strictness. In the Irish monasteries the monks, when at home, lived in separate cells, and when abroad preached the Gospel as missionaries. In the Benedictine monastery, the monks lived, prayed, and slept together in common. They were celebrated for their learning, and built fine churches ; they cultivated the waste lands and were good farmers ; they gave shelter to the scholar, and the artist, and in a rough and turbulent age, the cloak of religion was a better protection than the sword.

Here is the rent which the Abbot of Medeshamstede (Peterborough) charged for land that he let to Wilfred, " each year should deliver into the minster sixty loads of wood, and twelve of coal and six of faggots, and two tuns full of pure ale, and two beasts fit for slaughter, and six hundred loaves, and ten measures of Welsh ale, and each year a horse, and thirty shillings, and one day's entertainment." This is an interesting passage because it shows that, though the usual method of trade was to barter commodities, yet money was in use as a means of exchange.

The Sceatta currency, and the Northumbrian styca, came before the penny first struck by Offa of Mercia. A wonderful find was made in 1840, of a leaden chest near a ford over the Ribble, above Preston. It contained 10,000 silver coins, and nearly 1,000 ozs. of silver ; it is thought to have been the treasure chest of the Danes who were defeated here in 911. Coins have been found at Rome of Offa, 757-96, and may have been " Peter's Pence."

Church Dues   Church dues were a very heavy charge on industry in these early days. Canute wrote to Ethelnoth, to take care that " all dues owing to ancient custom be discharged : that is to say, plough-alms (a penny to the poor for as much land as a plough could till), the tenth of animals born in the current year, and the pence owing to Rome for S. Peter ; and in the middle of August the tenth of the produce of the earth ; and on the festival of S. Martin, the first fruits of the seeds (a sack of corn from every load), to the church and the parish where each one resides." People complain of high taxation in these days, but here was an Income Tax, not on the profit of the year, but the whole turn-over.

The Church gave very good value for the money received, because not only were the souls of the people saved, but their everyday life was regulated. Dunstan observed that " as his countrymen used to assemble in taverns, and when a little elevated quarrel as to the proportion of their liquor, he ordered gold or silver pegs to be fastened in the pots, that whilst every man knew his just measure, shame should compel each neither to take more himself nor oblige others to drink beyond their proportional share."

The Church at an early date encouraged pilgrimage. We read in the Chronicle (816) : " The same year the English School at Rome was burned." This was near S. Peter's, for the accommodation of pilgrims. These pilgrimages played their part in educating and interesting people, and as the Church of Rome has always been very democratic, the son of a peasant could become first priest, then prelate, and, going to

FIG. 59.—Tower of Sompting Church, Sussex.

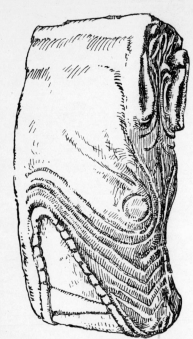

FIG. 60.—Carving, Deerhurst
Church, Gloucestershire.

Rome, come back and tell his friends of all the fine things he had seen there.

Aelfric is another of the churchmen who have left us a picture of Saxon times. He was a monk in the New-minster (Winchester), founded in the time of Eadgar (958-975). He tells of the ranks into which the people were divided, and it is evident that by his time there was less freedom than there had been. We have seen how in Alfred's time it became necessary to put the safety of the State before the comfort of the people, as it was with us in 1914-1918. Formerly the main division was between

Eorles and Ceorles

" eorles " and " ceorles," or gentle and simple, but if the " ceorl " thrived and had five hides of land, a church, kitchen, and a place in the king's hall, then he became worthy of Thane-right, and so could the merchant and the thane become an " eorl."

Aelfric, in his " Colloquies," tells us of the duties of men, and these by the time of Canute had been so regulated, that every man had his job and definite position in the State. The Thegn held his land on condition that he rendered military service, and undertook the repair of fortifications, and bridge building. The Geneat, Cottar, and Gebur, were retainers, or tenants, of the Thegn, or lord, and held their land on condition that they supported him. Th e Beekeeper, Swineherd, Oxherd, Cowherd, Shepherd, Goatherd, Cheesemaker, Barnman, Beadle,

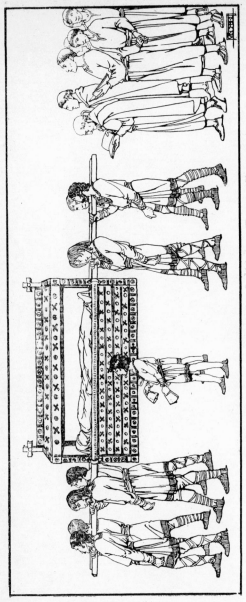

Fig. 61.—Funeral of Edward the Confessor. (Bayeux Tapestry.)

Woodward, Hayward and the Sowers all had their dues and duties defined. The keepers of animals had to guard them as well. Edgar " commanded Judwall, king of the Welsh, to pay him yearly a tribute of three hundred wolves." The slaves were not forgotten. A slave woman was entitled to eight pounds of corn for food, one sheep or three pennies for winter food, one sester of beans for Lenten fare, and in summer whey, or one penny. As well they were entitled to a feast at Christmas, and another at Easter, and a handful of corn at harvest beside their other dues. We do not know if Canute himself laid down these rules. In them it is stated that though customs varied, those mentioned were the general ones, yet if better could be found they would be gladly approved.

In viewing these customs ourselves we must not condemn them too hastily as having been based on slavery. The system was very closely knit and strong because it was based on the land. Our own world, for little more than a century, which, historically speaking, is only a flicker of time, has toyed with the ideas of freedom and liberty, and an industrial system which is weak because it is divorced from the land. To-day whole classes of people are dependent on others for their schooling and books ; have to be assisted to build houses, and have baths, and receive doles when they are unemployed, and subsidies when trade is bad, and we import nearly all our food. If Canute could have contrasted our customs with his own he might not have been greatly chagrined.

Perhaps the final note in this part should be one on the spread of knowledge which made possible the developments of the next period. William of Malmesbury tells of the training of Pope Silvester (1002), who travelled among the Saracens in the South of Spain. He practised the use of the astrolabe for making celestial observations, became skilled in astronomy and astrology ; he acquired the art of calling up spirits from hell—arithmetic, music and geometry ; learned to use the abacus or counting table. Later in Gaul, when Archbishop of Rheims, he constructed a clock on " mechanical principles, and an hydraulic organ, in which the air, escaping in a surprising manner, by the force of heated water, fills the cavity of the instrument, and the brazen pipes emit modulated tones through the multifarious apertures."

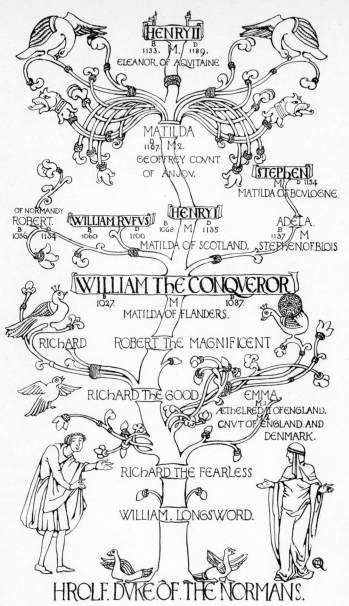

HENRY II
B 1133. M. D 1189.
ELEANOR OF AQVITAINE

MATILDA
B 1157. M 2.
GEOFFREY COVNT
OF ANJOV.

STEPHEN
M D 1154
MATILDA OF BOVLOGNE.

OF NORMANDY.
ROBERT.
B 1056. 1134.

WILLIAM RVFVS
B 1060. D 1100.

HENRY I
B 1068. M. D 1135.
MATILDA OF SCOTLAND.

ADELA.
B 1137. M
STEPHEN.OF.BLOIS

WILLIAM THE CONQVEROR
B 1027. M 1087.
MATILDA OF FLANDERS.

RICHARD   ROBERT THE MAGNIFICENT

RICHARD THE GOOD   EMMA
M.I.
ÆTHELRED II OF ENGLAND.
CNVT OF ENGLAND. AND
DENMARK.

RICHARD THE FEARLESS

WILLIAM. LONGSWORD.

HROLF. DVKE. OF. THE. NORMANS.

FIG. 62.

N

CHAPTER III

THE COMING OF THE NORMANS

N this chapter we arrive at the period with which we started in Part I of a "History of Everyday Things in England." In that book we dealt with the appearance of the Norman people and their ships, castles, monasteries, cathedrals, games, and general customs. We shall not, therefore, cover the same ground again, but seek for new types so that the two books may be complementary one to the other.

We think that the more the Normans are studied the greater respect one has for their energy and intelligence, but it needs some explanation that so much became possible to them. They were of the same Nordic type as the Saxons and Vikings, and it was as the Northmen, or Norsemen, that they settled in Normandy, under Hrolf, in 912, and, as we showed on page 68, very unpleasant neighbours the French found them.

It will be well, at this point, for boys and girls to check their historical perspective. To-day, quite properly, they think with pride of England as the homeplace of a great commonwealth of free nations, but it was not so in ancient times. In the Bronze Age England was El Dorado, and men sought gold here. In the Roman Empire we took the place of a troublesome north-west province, with Scots, Picts and Saxons to hamper and fret the Romanized Britons, and in the later Anglo-Saxon invasions the whole country sank back into anarchy and confusion. France was spared many of these troubles. The Roman Empire was more firmly established in Gaul than in our island, and better able to withstand the Franks who invaded them, and the Roman Gauls had this great advantage, that their enemies, whose leader, Clovis, was

baptized in 496, became
Christians 100 years be-
fore Augustine appeared
on our shores to convert
the men of Kent; so in
Gaul men settled down
and made good the
damage of the inva-
sions, long before we
were able to do the
same. In this way they
were more prepared for
the later Viking raids
than we were, and the
Normans were the only
northern people who
were able to obtain any
foothold in France, and

FIG. 63.—Carpenter.

here again they did not work so much destruction as our
Vikings. The Normans appear to have been content to settle
down in Normandy and benefit by the civilization of their
neighbours, instead of destroying it. Like Alfred, they were
curiously eager to investigate things unknown.

We will now try to find out what kind of people they were. Master
Our principal authority will be Master Wace and his Chronicle Wace
of the Norman Conquest from the Roman de Rou. Wace
was a trouvère or troubadour at the court of Henry II, and
his sprightly tale forms an admirable text to the pictures of
the Tapestry at Bayeux, which is another great record of the
Conquest.

Wace gives us a graphic picture of life in Normandy when
William was forging the sword with which to conquer England.
His barons were turbulent, and before they could be welded
into a whole by feudalism had to be persuaded to leave off
killing one another. The Truce of God was introduced by
William, in 1061, and enforced by him as a restraint on the
Normans. " He made all swear on the relics to hold peace
and maintain it from sunset on Wednesday to sunrise on
Monday. This was called the TRUCE, and the like of it I
believe is not in any country. If any man should beat another
meantime, or do him any mischief, or take any of his goods,

Fig. 64.—The Building of William's Fleet. (Bayeux Tapestry.)

FIG. 65.—William's Sappers.

he was to be excommunicated, and amerced nine livres to the bishop."

Harold, on his way to Normandy, was taken prisoner by the Count of Ponthieu, and delivered up to William, who thus appeared to come to Harold's rescue. He was nobly entertained by the Duke, and then trapped into promising to deliver England to the Norman on the death of Edward. To receive the oath, William caused a Parliament to be called. As well, " He sent for all the holy bodies thither, and put so many of them together as to fill a whole chest, and then covered them with a pall ; but Harold neither saw them, nor knew of them being there ; for nought was shown or told to him about it ; and over all was a phylactery, the best that he could select ; oeil de boeuf, I have heard it called. When Harold placed his hand upon it, the hand trembled, and the flesh quivered ; but he swore, and promised upon his oath to take Ele to wife, and to deliver up England to the duke . . . when Harold . . . had risen upon his feet, the duke led him up to the chest, and made him stand near it ; and took off the chest the pall that had covered it, and shewed Harold upon what holy relics he had sworn, and he was sorely alarmed at the sight."

Harold's Oath

93

Fig. 66.—Mount-and-Bailey Castle. (Reconstruction from Bayeux Tapestry.)

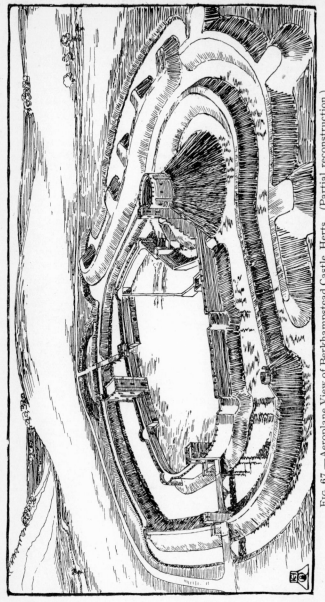

Fig. 67.—Aeroplane View of Berkhampstead Castle, Herts. (Partial reconstruction.)

FIG. 68.—William's Army Cooks.

We can read in Wace how, when Harold failed to keep his promise, the preparations for the conquest went forward. William received gifts and promises of men and ships ; the old Viking spirit of adventure came into play again, and the signs were auspicious. "Now while these things were doing, a great star appeared, shining for fourteen days, with three long rays streaming towards the south ; such a star as is wont to be seen when a kingdom is about to change its king." So there was great enthusiasm. William "got together carpenters, smiths, and other workmen, so that great stir was seen at all the ports of Normandy, in the collecting of wood and materials, cutting of planks, framing of ships and boats, stretching sails and rearing masts, with great pains and at great cost. They spent all one summer and autumn in fitting up the fleet and collecting the forces."

Then the time came when they were ready to sail, and "they prayed the convent to bring out the shrine of S. Valeri, and set it on a carpet in the plain ; and all came praying the holy reliques, that they might be allowed to pass over sea. They offered so much money, that the

FIG. 69.—William's Army Cooks.

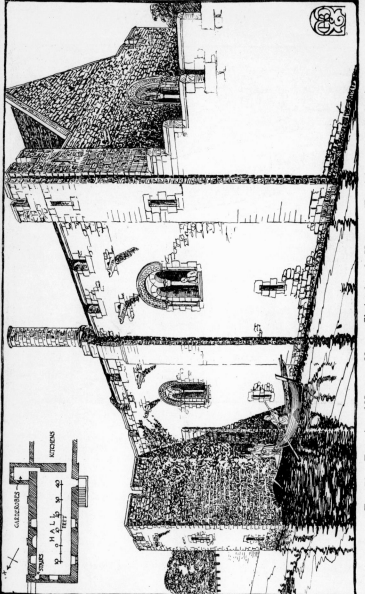

FIG. 70.—Exterior of Norman House, Christchurch, Hants. (Partial reconstruction.)

o

Fig. 71.—The Hall of the Norman House, Christchurch, Hants.
(Partial reconstruction.)

reliques were buried beneath it; and from that day forth, they had good weather and a fair wind."

Wace tells how " I heard my father say—I remember it well, although I was but a lad—that there were seven hundred ships, less four, when they sailed from S. Valeri; and that there were besides these ships, boats and skiffs for the purpose of carrying the arms and harness," and when at length they started, "The Duke placed a lantern on the mast of his ship, that the other ships might see it, and hold their course after it."

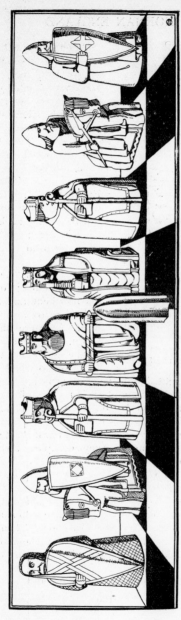

Fig. 72.—Chessmen found at Uig, Isle of Lewis, carved in Morse Ivory. Twelfth Century. (British Museum.)

Norman
Landing

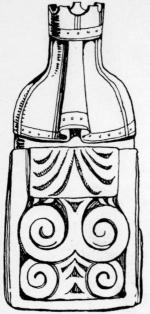

FIG. 73.—Back of the Queen.

When they reached England, "As the ships were drawn to shore, and the Duke first landed, he fell by chance upon his two hands. Forthwith all raised a loud cry of distress, 'an evil sign,' said they, 'is here.' But he cried out lustily, 'See, seignors, by the splendour of God! I have seized England with my two hands; without challenge no prize can be made; all is our own that is here; and now we shall see who is the bolder man.'"

The archers "touched the land foremost; each with his bow bent and his quiver full of arrows slung at his side. All were shaven and shorn, and all clad in short garments, ready to attack, to shoot, to wheel about and skirmish. The knights landed next, all armed; with their hauberks on, their shields slung at their necks, and their helmets laced. They formed together on the shore, each armed upon his warhorse. All had their swords girded on, and passed into the plain with their lances raised. The barons had gonfanons, and the knights pennons. They occupied the advanced ground, next to where the archers had fixed themselves. The carpenters, who came after, had great axes in their hands, and planes and adzes at their sides. When they had reached the spot where the archers stood, and the knights were assembled, they consulted together, and sought for a good spot to place a strong fort upon. Then they cast out of the ships the materials and drew them to land, all shaped, framed and pierced to receive the pins which they had brought, cut and ready in large barrels; so that before evening had well set in, they had finished a fort. Later a

100

knight describes how " he saw them build up and enclose a fort, and dig the fosse around it," and how " they strengthened it round about with palisades and a fosse."

The castle which Wace describes is similar to that shown on the Bayeux Tapestry, which we illustrate in Fig. 66. It is called now the Mount-and-Bailey type. The Mount was formed by scarping down a natural hill, or raising an artificial one with the earth dug out of the ditches. On this the fort was built and surrounded by a timber palisade. The ditch of the mount was taken as well round the bailey, and here were the stables, barns, kitchens, and barracks. The site always included

Castles

FIG. 74.—Back of the King.

a good spring of water. In such a castle William could leave a garrison to hold down the countryside. The Saxons had nothing so scientific at their disposal. Just as the Viking with his ship as a base, and his horse to carry him about, could deliver a blow at his own time, so the Normans, in the security of their castles, could select the moment for attack.

William knew all about building stone castles. Wace tells us how William of Arques built a tower above Arches (Chateau d'Arques, near Dieppe), and was besieged there by Duke William. The King of France came to the assistance of William of Arques, and Duke William, hearing of his intention, " strengthened his castles, cleaning the fosses, and repairing the walls. . . . Caen was then without a castle, and had neither wall nor fence to protect it." Stone

Fig. 75.—The Knight.

walls are evidently meant here and differentiated from wooden fences or palisades. William built timber castles at first in England because they could be constructed quickly.

We can now return to the details of the Conquest, and as the pages of Wace are read one becomes very sorry for the Saxons; they were beaten by the most wonderful staff work. William not only brought over castles packed in casks, but remembered that armies march on their stomachs. Wace tells how "you might see them make their kitchens, light their fires, and cook their meat. The duke sat down to eat, and the barons and knights had food in plenty; for he had brought ample store. All ate and drank enough, and were right glad that they were ashore."

The Bayeux tapestry shows the Normans arriving at Pevensey, but according to Wace they first landed near Hastings and William "ordered proclamation to be made, and commanded the sailors that the ships should be dismantled, and drawn ashore and pierced, that the cowards might not have the ships to flee to." This can only be regarded as a gesture to his men that they must do or die. William would hardly have cut off his line of retreat, or have built a fort at Hastings, except to leave a garrison in it to safeguard the fleet.

His next step was to move west about 12 miles to Pevensey. "The English were to be seen fleeing before them, driving off their cattle, and quitting their houses. All took shelter in the cemeteries, and even there they were in grievous alarm." Here again is evidence of staff work. Pevensey

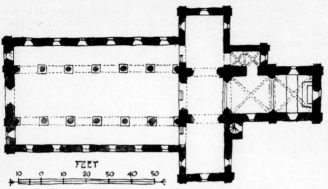

FIG. 76.—Plan of Hemel Hempstead Church, Herts.

was one of the forts built about 300 A.D. by the Romans to protect the east and south coasts from the Saxon raids (see Part 3, page 91). As the Roman walls with their bastions enclosing several acres are still standing to-day, they must, in William's time, have formed a good strong base where he could be safe and so compel Harold to come to him.

This was what poor Harold had to do. He came post haste from the Humber, from his encounter with Tosti, first to London, and then south again, and " erected his standard and fixed his gonfanon right where the Abbey of the Battle is now built," about 9 miles away from William at Pevensey. Here Harold dug himself in. " He had the place well examined and surrounded it by a good fosse, leaving an entrance on each of the three sides, which were ordered to be all well guarded."

We shall not concern ourselves very much with the details of the fighting, but there is one very interesting detail which must be noted. In the old Viking days, and the tale of Burnt Njal, fighting is mentioned quite casually, as fishing might be, or hunting. It was undertaken as a sport. From the time of the Normans onwards people sought to justify themselves. There were many parleys in 1066, and much talk of the justice of the respective causes. Each side appealed for the favour of Heaven, and there were threats of the dire consequences which would befall the opponent. The combatants, like modern boxers, reassured themselves, and their backers, and appear to have stood in need of support. When William " prepared to arm himself, he called first for his good hauberk, and a man brought it on his arm and placed it before him ; but in putting his head in to get it on, he inadvertently turned it the wrong way, with the back part in front. He quickly changed it, but when he saw that those who stood by were sorely alarmed, he said, ' I have seen many a man who, if such a thing happened to him, would not have borne arms or entered the field the same day ; but I never believed in omens, and I never will. I trust in God.' "

One of Harold's spies, who had seen the Normans, reported that they " were so close shaven and cropt, that they had not even moustaches, supposed he had seen priests and mass-sayers; and he told Harold that the duke had more priests with him than knights or other people." But Harold replied, " Those are valiant knights, bold and brave warriors, though they bear not beards or moustaches as we do." William's priests were quite prepared to be useful. " Odo, the good priest, the bishop of Bayeux, ' was always found ' where the battle was most fierce, and was of great service on that day."

After the battle, " The English who escaped from the field did not stop till they reached London." Again there is evidence of wonderful staff work. William did not at once pursue the enemy, but turned his attention to consolidating his position.

We will now ask our readers to refer to the map, Fig. 3, in Part III of this series, or the much better one of Roman Britain published by the Ordnance Survey. It will be seen why William selected Hastings as his point of attack. Pevensey was close by, and all by itself and so more vulnerable. On the other hand, the usual entrance into England, by Watling Street, was protected by a group of forts at Lympne, Folkestone, Dover, Richborough, and Reculver. Some of these must have been in repair, because we read in Wace, of how William went back east to Romney, which he destroyed, and then on to Dover. Obviously some Norman troops had been detailed to hold the English in check, and prevent them coming to the assistance of Harold, because Wace says that William did not rest " till he reached Dover, at the strong fort he had ordered to be made at the foot of the hill."

Here he besieged the old Roman fort, and though the place was well fortified, took it after an eight-day siege. William placed a garrison in it, and was now ready for the great adventure ; he had won a great battle ; could he hold the country ?

Canterbury rendered homage and delivered hostages to the Conqueror, who then journeyed to London. Arrived at Southwark, the citizens issued out of the gates, but were speedily driven back, and the Normans burned all the houses on the south side of the Thames. Here again William gave another proof of genius. He had given the Londoners a taste of his quality, and his most urgent need was to thrust a spear head in between his enemies before they had the opportunity to gather their forces together. This William did by going to Wallingford on the Thames, where it is thought that he crossed, and then passed by Icknield Way to the gap in the Chilterns at Tring, and then on to our own town of Great Berkhampstead. Again we will look at the map of Roman Britain and note that William's last raid gave him possession of many of the roads leading into London. First there was Stane Street from Portsmouth and Chichester. Then the very important road crossing the Thames at Staines, which branched off at Silchester into three roads serving the south and west. At Tring, William cut across Akeman Street, and could control Watling Street at Dunstable. The strategy was brilliantly successful, because the English surrendered and William received the crown of England in the grounds of Berkhampstead Castle. In any case, when we had our pageant at Berkhampstead, in 1922, the player who took the part of William was so invested.

We can now pass on to the work of the Normans when they were established in the country, and Fig. 67 shows a recon-truction of Berkhampstead Castle. It is supposed that the earthworks and the Mount are the work of Robert, Count of Mortain, who was in possession of Berkhampstead at the time of Domesday. Little remains now except these earthworks, and the few remaining walls are slowly but surely crumbling into ruin. It is a tragic ending for a building which has seen so much history, and housed so many famous men. Henry I came to Berkhampstead in 1123, and Thomas Becket was in charge of the works between 1156-1160.

Edward III and the Black Prince held their Courts within its walls. Froissart was another inhabitant, and Geoffrey Chaucer another clerk of the works. To-day it is neglected and forlorn. Children scramble over the banks, and goats crop the grass in the Bailey.

Shell Keep

The plan is of great interest because it shows the development of what is called the Shell Keep. As the artificial mounts became consolidated, the timber forts, as Fig. 66, were replaced with a stone wall. At Berkhampstead, Fig. 67, when the Mount was excavated, it was discovered that this Shell was about 60 feet external diameter, the wall being 8 feet thick. There would have been a rampart walk on the top of this, and various sheds around it inside. There were steps up the Mount, and these were protected by a tower at the top, and by the moat or ditch being taken around the Mount at the base. The Bailey had an inner and outer ward, and these were surrounded by flint rubble walls about 7 feet thick, of which some few parts remain. These had bastions and gates as shown, and were further protected by the two ditches and bank between, which make the castle so interesting.

The next development of the castle is shown in Part I of *Everyday Things in England*, pages 11-19.

Norman House

We will now describe one of the most interesting buildings in England, the Norman House at Christchurch, Hants, the ruins of which are situated in the Garden of the King's Head Hotel. The important detail to remember is that the English house started its life as a hall. On page 18 we have given a description of the hall in Beowulf, but here at Christchurch we can leave literary evidence behind, and look at the actual stones of an early twelfth century house. It started life as the hall of the castle, and was built between 1125-1150. In Beowulf the hall is obviously on the ground floor level, but at Christchurch it has been moved to the first floor. This gave more sense of security, and enabled the windows to be bigger than would have been possible on the level of the ground. These had no glass, only wooden shutters for use at night. The hall was to remain on the first floor until life became a little more secure, in the fourteenth century, when it was moved downstairs, as at Penshurst.

Unfortunately the very considerable remains at Christchurch are so swathed with ivy, that the walls are not only being

FIG. 77.—The Interior of Hemel Hempstead Church, Herts. (Partial
reconstruction.)

P 2

destroyed, but it is very difficult to form any idea of what the building used to look like. However, we have made a careful survey of the ruins, and Figs. 70 and 71 are our reconstructions. The plan is very simple, just one large hall on the first floor, where the family lived, ate, and slept, because there was nowhere else to go. One remarkable detail is that there is a good fireplace in the hall, yet side by side, the old custom of the fire in the centre of the hall was to remain till as late as 1570 at the Middle Temple Hall. At Christchurch the kitchens came at the S..end of the hall, where also were the garderobes or lavatories. At the N. end was a circular staircase, which led up to the ramparts and down to a large room on the level of the ground, where doubtless men-at-arms and stores were. Then, of course, there would have been many sheds, stables, and barns, in the Castle Bailey, which was surrounded by a wall. The house was built as part of this wall, so that the inhabitants could look across the mill stream, to which access was gained by a water gate, shown in Fig. 70. If our readers are interested in the development of the house plan, we should like to refer them to Part I of *Everyday Things in England*, where we have shown how other rooms were gradually grouped around the hall, until, in the fifteenth century, the hall had become a house as we understand it.

Chessmen Figs. 72, 73 and 74 are of a magnificent set of chessmen in the King Edward Gallery at the British Museum. They are carved in morse ivory and were found at Uig in the Isle of Lewis. They date from the twelfth century. The people in the hall at Christchurch may have played chess with chessman like these. The king stands 4 inches high. The warders, one biting his shield in rage, which take the place of the castles, should be noted.

Now we are approaching the end of our task, and with superb artistry have kept the really triumphant achievement of the Normans for our finale. Unless we are careful, we look back and think only of their castles ; we may have been to the Tower of London, or have caught sight of Rochester on our way along that very old way, Watling Street, or we may have been to Castle Hedingham, Essex. These three wonderful Keeps may have oppressed our spirits, as they did the Saxons who were held in thrall under their walls.

Fig. 78.—Exterior of Hemel Hempstead Church, Herts. (Partial reconstruction.)

FIG. 79.—Chancel Vaulting, Hemel Hempstead Church, Herts.

Stare, stark, and strong, these great walls rear themselves up, yet they are full of delightful little bits of detail which gladden the architect. Judged only by their castles, the Normans would seem too fierce and formidable, but when we come to their cathedrals, and churches, there is a very different tale to tell. The architecture is still fierce and proud. It lacks the grace of the thirteenth century, and makes you think of a race of priests who could challenge kings and usurers. Abbot Samson, of whom Carlyle wrote in *Past and Present*, and Becket were of the same breed, turbulent, but very strong, and not given to compromise or half measures in their fight against evil. There is hardly a cathedral in England in which their hand cannot be traced, and their vision and grasp of planning was superb ; it was almost as if they took William's favourite oath as their motto and built to the " Splendour of God."

Norman Church

We have selected for our illustrations, not a cathedral, but the Church of Hemel Hempstead, Herts, which shows how the Normans went to work when they wanted to build a parish church in a small market town about 1140.

We will ask our readers first to study the plan, Fig. **74**, and as the majority of them, we hope, will be boys and girls who want to do creative work, they must acquire, in a very un-English way, the habit of liking plans. All buildings, all engineering work, all paintings, and sculpture, are built up on plans, or lay-outs, and the plan settles the structure ; it is the skeleton. A bad plan means inevitably a bad building ; one which has not been thought out ; it will be crippled and mis-shapen, and these faults will not be redeemed by any amount of detail, no matter how beautiful.

The plan Fig. 76 shows that the men of Hemel Hempstead, in 1140, understood the value of a simple lay-out of cruciform type, and Fig 77 how this resolved itself into a wonderful interior, in which one looked through darkness into light. Fig. 78 is the exterior. Our illustrations have been made from sketches of the actual building, and the few liberties we have taken, have only been in the way of eliminating later work, and restoring the Norman detail ; internally, we have omitted the modern " Gothic " choir stalls, and externally the later leaded spire is not shown on the Norman tower, and so on. The church has, fortunately for us, escaped the vandalism of the nineteenth century in a surprising fashion.

Fig. 79 shows the vaulting to the chancel, and is an amusing example of how the old masons played with the problems of solid geometry. The Normans at first used the plain semi-circular barrel vault. Then one day somebody made two of these vaults cross as A (Fig. 79), but the result did not satisfy them for long, because the intersections, or groins, at B, were necessarily flatter than a semi-circle ; they had to be, because their span was greater than that of the vault, and they had to spring, and finish, at the same levels. So the next step was to make the groin itself semi-circular, as shown in the main drawing of Fig. 79 at C. Then the cross ribs at D had to be raised up on legs, or stilted, to reach to the height of the groins. This was really a little clumsy, so the cross rib was turned into a pointed arch, but that is another story which is told in Part I of *Everyday Things in England*, where we show how step by step the old masons progressed up to the glorious fan vaulting of Henry the VII's Chapel at Westminster Abbey.

<small>Vaulting</small>

If this church at Hemel Hempstead is compared with those of the Anglo-Saxons we have illustrated, it will be noted how great an advance the Normans made in the art of building ; there is no fumbling with their work, but a splendid self-confidence. They were a wonderful people and their stock first comes into notice with the Norsemen, or Northmen, who raided our land as Vikings. They played a great part here in Saxon times, and, as we noted on page 84, the majority of the churches we now call Anglo-Saxon are found in the parts of the country in which the Vikings settled. We must bear in mind their travels to the East through

Russia; their discoveries by land, and their adventures by sea. They were a people, and it is a period, to which far more detailed study should be given than is possible in this little book.

England has welcomed many men. The Piltdown Man of the Old Stone Age, and the Mediterranean men of the New Stone Age; the Goidels or Gaels; the Brythons or Britons, and the Belgae. Rome and her legionaries brought blood from all over Europe. Then came the Angles, Saxons, and Jutes; the Vikings and Normans; the Angevins, Flemings, Huguenots, and all the other oddments who have drifted in. Age after age the soil of our island has attracted men; here they have lived, and dying, their bones or ashes have been turned into the soil of England. Each in their turn have made their contribution to the common stock, and the genius of the race, and the Viking, Norseman, or Norman, was not the least of these men. It may well be that England will go forward just so long as their courage and love of adventure are not allowed to be swamped by the vulgar chaffering of the market place.

And here our task ends. Farewell.

Fig. 80.—Head of Tau—Cross of Walrus Ivory, found at Alcester, Warwickshire. Early Eleventh Century. (British Museum.)

INDEX TO TEXT AND ILLUSTRATIONS

NOTE.— *The ordinary figures denote references to pages of text; those in black type, the illustrations.*

A

Aelfric, 86
Aidan, 8, 46
Alb, 16
S. Alban, 8
Alfred, 7, 16, 67
Angles, 4, 7, 32
Anglo-Saxons, 8, 9, 10
Anglo-Saxon Chronicle, 7
Armenia, 40
Arms, **11**
Arthur, 7, 36
Athelstan, 16
Attila, 5
Augustine, 39, 40, 41, 51

B

Baptism, 42
Barn, **23,** 26
Baths, 3
Bayeux Tapestry, 91, 102
Bed, **61, 63**
Bede, 4, 16, 35
Belgae, 1
Bells, 82
S. Benedict, 83
S. Benet's Church, **79,** 80
Beowulf, 18
Berkhampstead Castle, **95,** 105
Bertha, 41
Biscop, 4
Boar, 11
Bosham, 49
Bottle, 27
Bradford-on-Avon, **70, 71, 72,** 80
Britain, 16
Britons, 1, 8, 17
Brooches, 11, **13,** 14
Brython, 1
Bucket, 33
Building, 75
Burgs, 63
Burial, 31
Burnt Njal, 56

C

Caedmon, 35
Candles, 31, **76**
Carpenter, **91,** 100
Carucates, 64
Cassino (Monte), 83
Castles, **94, 95,** 100, 101
Ceorl, 14
Charlemagne, 34
Chasuble, 16
Chessmen, **99, 100, 101, 102,** 108
Christ (Figure of), **50**
Christchurch, 106
Clock, 88
Columba, 8, 46
Combats, 77
Cooks, 96
Cope, 16
Costume, Fig, 11, 10
Cottar, 86
Cremation, 32
Cro-magnon, 1
Crooks, 26
Crosses, 41, **55,** 83, **112**
Crucks, 26
Cup, 31, **41**

D

Dalmatic, 16
Danelaw, 63, 72, 77
David, **7**
Deerhurst, **86**
Derby, 63
Domesday, 10, 64
Dooms, 10
Dragon, 22
Dues, 84
Dunstan, 76, 77
Durham Book, 37

E

Earls Barton, **73, 56,** 80
Easter, 40, 46, 51
Ebbsfleet, 7

INDEX TO TEXT AND ILLUSTRATIONS

Edessa, 40
Education, 34
Egbert, 7
Enclosures, 10
English, 17
Ephod, 15
Escomb, 41
Etheldrida, 33

F

Figure, **51**
Fireplace, 108
Fishing, 48
Font, **57**
Fort, 100
Franks, 5
Franks Casket, 38, **47**
Freemen, 10
Frey, 66
Funeral, **87**

G

Gael, 1
Games, 35
Gebur, 86
Genealogical Tree, **89**
Geneat, 86
Giants, 36
Gildas, 36
Glass, **30, 31,** 32
Gokstad Ship, **60, 62**
Goths, 5
Grasslands, 5
Graves, 31
Greek, 35
Greek Church, 49
Gregory (Pope), 43
Gospels of S. Chad, **46**
Gospels of Durrow, **8**
Grendel, 20
Grimbald Gospels, 38

H

Hall, Frontispiece, 9, 18, **21,**
    24, **25,** 76, **98,** 106
Helmet, 11
Hemel Hempstead, **103, 107,**
    109, 110
Hengest, 6
Heorot, 20
History, 35

Holy Isle, 8, 49
Homestead, **19**
Horn, **43**
Houses, 26, **97,** 98
Hrothgar, 20
Hundreds, 77
Hygelac, 22

I

Illuminating, 37
Inhumation, 32
Inn, 10
Iona, 8, 46

J

Javelins, 12
S. John, **5**
Jug, **37**
Jutes, 4, 7, 14, 31

K

Kells (Book of), **6,** 37, **44**
Knick-knacks, **17**

L

Lantern, 76
Latin, 35
Latins, 17
Leicester, 63
Liber Vitae, 38
Lincoln, 63
Lindisfarne Gospels, 37, **45**
London, 18, 75
Looms, 15
S. Luke, **5**

M

Mail, 11
Manuscripts, 36
S. Mark, **3, 4, 9**
The Mark, 10
S. Martin's Church, 42
S. Matthew, **4**
Medicine, 33
Mediterranean Man, 1
Mellitus, 18
Mensuration, 28
Mill, 10
Mohammed, 6
Monasticism, 83
Money, 84
Moot Hill, 10
Mount and Bailey Castle, **94**

INDEX TO TEXT AND ILLUSTRATIONS

N

Necklaces, 12
New Minster, 38, 86
Nords, 1
Normans, 90
Norman House, **97, 98,** 106
Nottingham, 63

O

Odin, 66
Ogham Characters, 39
Ohthere, 74
Organ, 88
Orosius, 74

P

Pall, 49
Pantheon, 43
S. Patrick, 8, 37, 40
Paulinus, 42, 46, **82**
" Peter's Pence," 84
Picts, 17
Pilgrimage, 84
Pillow-stones, 33
Pins, 14
Plagues, 34
Plough Alms, 84
Pole or Perch, **27**. 29
Pottery, 31, 32

R

Rent, 83
Richborough, 7
Rod, **27,** 29
Roofs, **21**
Runes, 38

S

Sappers, **93**
Saxons, 2, 4, 7, 32
Scots, 17
Scramasaxe, 12, 38
Scriptorium, 37
Scyld, 20
Seals, 39, **49**
Selsey, 49
Shell Keep, **95,** 106
Shield, **12**
Ships, **59, 60, 62,** 75, 78, **92**
Sigebert, 34
Silchester, 2, 40

Sompting, **81,** 82, **85**
Spear, 11
Stamford, 63
Swastika, 83
Symbols, 82
Synod of Whitby, 40

T

Table-furniture, 30
Tapestries, 20
Tau-Cross, **112**
Temples, 43
Thane, 10, 86
Thanet, 7
Theodore, 34
Thing, 64
Thor, 66
Timber-framing, 24
Toga, 16
Tombstones, 33
Trajan Column, 10
Triclinium, 3
Trithings, 64
Truce of God, 91
Tumblers, **30, 31**

U

Urn, **29,** 32, **35**
Urnes Church, **52, 53**
Utrecht Psalter, 38

V

Valhal, 67
Valkyrie, 67
Vaulting, **110,** 111
Vikings, 56
Visigoths, 6

W

Wace, 91
Wapentakes, 64
Wealhtheow, 20
Weaving, 15
Wedmore (Peace of), 63, 72
Wilfrid, 33, 48
William, 91
Wing, **64, 65, 66, 67,** 78, 80
Witan, 76
Work-box, 15
Worth, 41, **68, 69,** 80
Writing Tablet, 39, **48**